The Love Crucible

Susan Lindsay

First published in 1995 by
Marino Books
An imprint of Mercier Press
16 Hume Street Dublin 2

Trade enquiries to Mercier Press
PO Box 5, 5 French Church Street,
Cork

© Susan Lindsay 1995

ISBN 1 86023 013 X

10 9 8 7 6 5 4 3 2 1

A CIP record for this title is available
from the British Library

Cover painting by Robert Armstrong
Cover design by Bluett
Set by Richard Parfrey
Printed in Ireland by ColourBooks,
Baldoyle Industrial Estate, Dublin 13

Love is an alchemical process in which we are the material to be transmuted.

Thomas Moore, 1994

ACKNOWLEDGEMENTS

All books are to some extent autobiographical, in that the author's life experience influences and punctuates the written word. *The Love Crucible* is no different in this regard. While it would be impossible and inappropriate even to attempt to name all who have influenced and taught me in relation to love, I would like to acknowledge some particular influences with appreciation. Doing so in no way suggests that those mentioned would necessarily agree with the views stated in the book.

I deeply appreciate the love of my grandparents and parents. Acknowledgement is also due to those who contributed to my early experience of church, which was a very warm experience of community. Ruarc Gahan and his colleagues of the time taught me the value of idealism and respect because of the respect they accorded their pupils and the ideals they brought to their job. They introduced me to A. S. Neill, which I also appreciate. Many years after I had learned about Wilhelm Reich I discovered that he and Neill were correspondents and it turned out that there had been a link, hitherto unknown, between early and later educational influences of mine. Len Goodman introduced me to therapy and growth groups. He is a great teacher.

Without the support of John Lindsay – my partner in learning about relationships for the past twenty years – this book could not have been written. Ben and Emma Lindsay have taught me what it is to be a parent and inspire me to say anything I have to say that is worth saying.

Jo O'Donoghue invited me to write a simple book about love. Without that invitation and the knowledge that she would eventually edit whatever was written it would not have been undertaken nor completed.

Special thanks are due to Louise Holborow who typed the manuscript. She also, along with all my colleagues, gave me endless encouragement. Much of my thinking has been developed in conversations over several years with Ger Murphy, who has been both supporting and challenging – or are these really the same thing?

Many others have supported and taught me along the way. My last and special appreciation is for those who have been my clients and who have been willing to trust me enough to allow me to accompany them on part of their journey. Thank you to all of you who have been willing to share a moment with open hearts along the way.

Susan Lindsay, March 1995

CONTENTS

INTRODUCTION

Our world is so full of savagery, beauty, joy, grief, destruction, creativity, romance and degradation, so full of contradictions and confusion, that it is difficult for us to make sense of it. The one crucial process that can possibly transmute all the pain, torture, chaos and magnificence can be signified as a melting-pot, a crucible of love.

The further we go on our inner journey, the more we recover ourselves and the closer we get to any sense of wholeness, the nearer we seem to come to a nature that has a tendency towards love and compassion, or, to put it another way, the closer we come to discovering a greater capacity within ourselves for love and compassion.

World religions, while they vary in their beliefs about the path to be followed and describe the ultimate goal in different ways, share a view that is in harmony with seeing the essence of life as love and compassion. Recently an eminent scientist, David Bohm, commented on our universe: 'Ultimately you come to a field of energies pervaded by consciousness and having the nature of compassion and love'. (*Wholeness and the Implicate Order*, quoted in Fr Bede Griffiths' *A New Vision of Reality*.)

If love *is* our nature, then we, collectively, seem very

far from realising it, not only in the sense of becoming aware of ourselves as having loving natures, but also in the sense of materialising that love in our world. What then has gone wrong and what do we need to do to remedy the situation? We all want to be loved, to experience love and, ultimately, to share love, but we have to contend with our history, our beliefs and the situations within which we find ourselves. These too are crucibles we can use.

1

WHY DO WE NOT LOVE ONE ANOTHER?

When you think about yourself in relation to love, you might ask yourself questions such as these:

- How capable of loving do I feel?
- To what extent do I believe that others love and care for me?
- To what extent do I really believe that I deserve their love?

These questions may appear to be easy to answer but try to think a little more deeply about them.

You may 'know' you are very loving, or not so, but how in practice is this demonstrated? You may be good at doing things for others, or making yourself available; you may always do everything people ask of you. Or you may demonstrate your lovingness to yourself by an awareness that you have lots of friends, or are married, or care for parents, or look after your children. You may also be saying to yourself that you must not be very loving because you often feel frustrated with your children, or with people needing a lot from you. In fact, when you begin to look at this question, in some way you will have recognised certain feelings you have or ways you behave that show you how you love.

If you take it further you will probably realise that there are particular kinds of loving that are easy for you and other ways that are much more difficult. For example, if you are good at making yourself available, are you also able to say 'no' and to impose limits so that you do not set yourself up to resent the very people to whom you offer help?

When you question the quality of the love of others, whether or not they are loving may seem immediately obvious, or you may be unsure about the answer. Whichever is the case, you are using familiar criteria to make this judgement, learned through what you've been taught about love. You may recognise love that is expressed physically because your family was good at offering hugs or warm physical contact. So you feel loved when this contact is present and the absence of physical expressions of affection may make you feel unloved. On the other hand, you may experience that kind of physical contact as soppy or false and be more interested in other ways people behave, for example, how thoughtful they are about taking the needs of others into account in their relationships and how they show their appreciation.

How far can you go in appreciating yourself? Can you say you deserve the love, any love, you receive, or does that go against the grain? Have you a conviction that valuing yourself engenders pride and is therefore dangerous. Or can you take a quiet pride in your own sense of yourself?

As we begin to look at ourselves in these ways, we can build a little more awareness about how we think about love, both in relation to ourselves and to others. This kind of awareness is the first step – although it is one from which we can benefit repeatedly – in looking at what we need to heal ourselves, both to heal the scars of past experiences of feeling less than loved and to enable ourselves to learn to love more effectively.

Our awareness of our relationship with love also has strong implications for our relationship with life itself. The extent to which we can have confidence in life, have faith that things will work out and are able to trust people will be influenced by whether we have a basic sense of life as having a nourishing, sustaining quality or as something which is out to get us or which we need to control carefully.

Loving requires an open heart. Opening our heart makes us vulnerable. Think of a moment when you vividly experienced an open heart, a moment when you were deeply touched – maybe after the birth of your child, or being present at a moment of courage or beauty. It could also have been a moment of parting from someone you love, your open heart leaving you vulnerable as they walked away.

We open our hearts to people who are special to us and allow them to touch us. But much of the time we keep our hearts closed and protected. We are protecting ourselves from pain – mostly from the pain of rejection or the pain of feeling foolish, and wisely so at times.

Our environment is often harsh and unfriendly: people are brusque; music blares in the supermarkets; advertisements confront us at every turn; traffic rushes by and we are caught up in the swirl of busy lives. If we were to open ourselves to all the harshness around us, we would have difficulty in surviving. So we close ourselves and live at one or several removes from our feelings, encasing ourselves in sufficient armour to survive our everyday lives.

In personal relationships, too, we are under threat. We do not, for the most part, deal sensitively with one another. Put-downs are common, feelings are not respected, sarcasm is a common form of humour. Stiff upper lips seem to be valued to such a degree that it is a denigration to speak of someone as sensitive. We often go to the other extreme and become so insensitive that we don't expect people to have feelings at all. Even common courtesies are frequently not respected.

Contrast these abrasive cultural experiences with the experience of holding a small baby in your arms. The soft warm body is so obviously vulnerable that it evokes a desire to be gentle and to offer protection. But we may feel uncomfortable and stiff with the child, not knowing what to do, unable to allow ourselves to yield and soften in response. So we hand it on to someone else as quickly as possible to avoid acknowledging the inadequacy of our response. Our armour has become so effective that we no longer dare to experience the warmth and vulnerability the baby evokes in us.

When we can allow ourselves to be present to the baby, however, and feel its naked dependence on us, our hearts open with love. Looking at its wide-eyed stare, we may grieve our own loss of innocence, or at least wish that we could protect this child from the inevitable loss of innocence that will occur. We know instinctively, if we take the time to think about it, that this child deserves love.

We do not think about whether this child is acceptable; we accept it exactly as it is. We might wish it didn't have needs to be met – that it wouldn't cry or need nappy changes that demand action from us – but it is so obviously perfect just the way it is that it seems superfluous to state the fact that it is totally acceptable to us.

Yet this baby will not grow up knowing that it is a perfect human being just by virtue of being itself; nor will it grow up totally loved and accepted because it will not be fully loved and accepted unconditionally. Although we may love the child, we will be limited in our ability to offer that child the love and acceptance it needs. Depending on the history of its parents, and the circumstances of their present lives, the child will experience itself as loved and accepted to a greater or lesser degree. This will depend not only on the parents' ability to love and on the maturity of their loving but on their ability to communicate that love to the child.

Some degree of love and acceptance are minimum requirements for the survival of our infant selves. Without warmth and affection infants do not thrive. Despite this, it is amazing how little some of us do manage to survive on, but there is always a price to be paid when our early need for love is insufficiently met. To the extent that the child's need to experience unconditional love and affection is met, he or she will be secure and trusting enough to allow his or her own heart to remain open. As the heart closes, the core self is lost. As we experience criticisms and put-downs we close the heart for protection; hence it is more difficult to love unconditionally. Since none of us have had the full experience of unconditional love, we all fall short in our capacity to love, to a greater or lesser extent. Even were our hearts nourished so well in this way as to remain intact, thereby enabling us to remain in touch with the inner core of our being, we would have to learn as we grow to protect ourselves by closing down – or else suffer incalculable damage. The challenge is to have adequate defences to manage our living in this world of damaged people and yet to remain sufficiently trusting and open to be able to love.

I have used the phrase 'damaged people', which implies that the situation should be different. Perhaps it could be different but it is also true that the damage being talked about here is an intrinsic part of the way things are. We do not seem to be able to love one other enough to prevent this damage occurring. Parents have to contend with their own history when they parent: they have to contend with the degree of nourishment they have received in early childhood; with their history of family relationships, learning about relationships and all that entails, and with their life history of traumas and successes. Many parents overcome huge obstacles in their history, while others do not, and it is often difficult to explain why some who have suffered severely learn to parent well while others appear unable to do so.

Experience as a therapist – especially in groups – convinces me that 'to know all would be to forgive all' because when a person's story is made known *as they experienced it* then what was apparently incomprehensible becomes clear. In fact the more one knows of the history of people, the more miraculous appears their ability to survive.

Trees grow into different shapes as they adapt to the conditions they experience, such as the availability of light, the space available, the conditions of the ground, the weather. Similarly, humans grow into all kinds of shapes, some twisted and gnarled in many ways. Most make the best of what they are but what they are does in turn affect the people around them, including the infants and children in their care. They become part of the conditions which influence the way in which the people around them grow.

So the degree to which people are currently capable of loving – or for that matter, of receiving love – and the way in which they love are largely determined by the context of their lives and, of course, by the choices they make. To exercise choice, one has to understand clearly that choice is available and that understanding in itself is not part of everyone's history.

If our future experience is to be different, it will be because we have learnt to overcome more of our history by healing hurt and recovering our ability to love. Love is what makes the difference, and in our own gnarled or twisted way, we have to learn to express that love in whichever way each of us can. As we ground ourselves more deeply in love and express that love more fully in our lives, what is twisted may straighten and the energy bound up in separating the compartments within ourselves may be freed as more inner healing takes place and we reach a greater stage of wholeness. If so, then it is our alienation from our deepest being and hence from love itself that is our greatest problem.

Most of all, what seems to separate us from spirit, from

the soul of ourselves, is this separation from core self. This separation comes from an inability to accept and value ourselves, not just as people who behave in certain ways and do not behave in other ways, but as people of value in our own right just by virtue of being. It never ceases to amaze me that Christians, whose religion has as its core theme the central message of love, have so much difficulty appreciating the innate value, not only of others but of themselves. For far too long it has been assumed that we have no difficulty in loving ourselves and every difficulty in loving others. Perhaps it is this inability to accept the deepest parts of ourselves with genuine love and pride – as distinct from an egocentric inflated pride which is only another form of defence – that alienates us most from our souls and the love that is divine. It was once put to me that sin can be defined as 'that which separates us from God'. If so, then perhaps alienation from ourselves is the greatest 'sin' there is.

Until we can truly love and accept ourselves, the person we know, how can we even presume to say we can love another. Yet it is often true that it is in loving another that we grow to know and appreciate more of ourselves. When we are touched deeply by a connection with another, we may discover greater depths in ourselves than we were willing or able to touch in ourselves previously.

We might like things to be different – and through recovering the loving connection we may be able to make changes – but we first have to recognise the reality of the way things are.

People are alienated from their core selves. To some degree we all are. That is the human condition. It is part of the human condition to encapsulate ourselves – our core selves – in a container. Carl Jung called this container the 'persona'. It is spoken of as a mask, the person we present to the world, through which we relate one to another. This container is an essential part of what it means to be human. It expresses much of our personality. It is part of the condition of being embodied.

Let us think for a moment about that phrase 'being embodied'. As human beings we are 'beings' who are 'embodied'. It is a fundamental element of our existence that we live in and through a body, that we cannot live in this world without bodies. It may even seem nonsensical to talk about self separately from embodied self. This is central to the paradox of being human. We are nothing apart from our bodies yet we can have a sense of ourselves as someone living in a body – as in a container. The paradox is that both perceptions are true. In this reality 'I am' my body and have no existence apart from it. Yet on another level of reality 'I' exist apart from my body: the essence of me has a life beyond my embodied existence. Perhaps at the death of my body my essence will returns to the 'source' as a droplet to the ocean, or to another level of existence, call it 'heaven' or what you will. Perhaps this essential self will be reincarnated, embodied as another human being to continue its journey.

The difficulty is to hold these two realities in place: to acknowledge, value and live this embodied reality whilst also being mindful of another level of existence; a level of being, a level of mindfulness, a level of detachment which allows us live through our body in this reality whilst deepening an awareness of the part of ourselves that is beyond this reality. This way of mindfulness, being or detachment is sought through many forms of meditation. Some forms emphasise detachment which can lead us to try to deny the body. Others, such as various schools of yoga or Tai'Chi (from China) encourage meditation paths which incorporate the body and through breathing and an awareness of the energy pathways of the body, lead both into our body experience and beyond it.

We have been invited, by virtue of our embodiment, to enter into the reality of being human. It seems vital, therefore, to enter fully into the experience if one is to get the most from what it has to offer.

Hence the challenge is to be present, as fully as possible, here in this reality. *To be present*: such simple words, so easy to take one's own presence for granted. Most of the time we are at most, half-present – away in our heads, preoccupied, living with thoughts, images, feelings. How often do we manage to be fully present: to be present in the particular moment with the whole of ourselves, present in our bodies, with attention for the moment, connected through our bodies to the deepest self and to others and the earth we live on.

Yet in our absences, we are absent to others: absent to ourselves and absent to the source of human beings; absent to love and to our ability to love one another.

This regular absence of self to oneself (and thereby to the inner source of oneself) and to others may shed some light on the Christian concept of original sin. Many people have huge difficulty with the notion of original sin as a theological proposition when it is put as an essential 'badness' (sin) that is part of one from birth and that has to be 'redeemed'. However, it might make sense if we thought of it in this way. If we reflect upon all the pressures we come under to be busy, to behave and think in particular ways, to be successful in certain ways, to make our bodies conform to particular expectations (of shape and posture), to be 'somebody', as distinct from being ourselves, then we cannot but be aware that there is very little space in our life to appreciate the sacredness of ourselves and others. The core of the person is not valued and the unique quality of each individual human being is given little attention. We live in a very disconnected way, disconnected from ourselves, from the inner wisdom of people, from nature and from the earth we live on and the ecosystem of which we are part.

Paradoxically, because of our very ability to control things, we, as a species, are out of control. All our emphasis seems to be on control and exploitation for our own needs, and we have little space for connectedness, for nature, for beauty, for quality, for love. We live alienated lives and have to remember to take special time to be. So we could say there has been a 'fall' (the Judeo-Christian religions talk of the 'fall from grace' that took place in the mythological Garden of Eden): a failure to remember who we are at core, a fall away from being connected, to being not only separate but separated.

We cannot talk about love as a state of separateness. It is a state of individuation, yes, that applies to the whole of yourself, but implies not separation from but connectedness to the depth of one's being, the universe, God or goddess, the Source, love itself. (The terms we use to describe the Divine tell us more about ourselves than the

ultimate divinity. It is important to remember that 'God"
is always more than any of the names we use, which
demonstrates the limitations of our vision. Hence the use
here of several names, which can be used interchangeably
hereafter). Love is always, by definition, part of relationship. Love is not an object, it is a part of being, being in
relationship. Although we can talk about love as a 'thing';
in fact we cannot describe or experience love except in
relationship. We cannot take love out of context. Love is
the energy that is almost the opposite of alienation, the
ultimate expression of being, while alienation, although
some way along the path to a place of non-existence is
not that place itself. Perhaps that is why many of the
mystics (of all religions) encourage us to enter the
blankness, or nothingness, the furthest point from love
that can be imagined, feared as a place of annihilation,
yet a place through which love so often emerges.

2

RECOVERING THE ABILITY TO LOVE

We have now recognised that love is central to our way of being in the world. It is a common experience – from the love of our parents, to the parenting we offer, to friendships, romance, marriage and the giving of ourselves, whether by being present fully to another or through acts of service.

Our experiences of love have a fundamental effect on the person we become. Perfect love is not the experience of most of us: perhaps it happens to no one. To the extent that we have experienced inadequate love and care and have been put down and injured, we will have been numbed or split off. We will be left as less than whole people. Similarly, if sufficient love has not been expected of us, our ability to be perceptive to the needs of others may not have grown.

As we develop in a world that is alien to a greater or lesser extent, our needs are met to one degree or another. The critical question for health and wellbeing is not whether our needs have been met but whether they have been met *well enough*. If we wish to be healthier – in its widest sense of wholeness – we need to heal the scars left by less than adequate loving. The first step is to realise that there are scars. Very often they are sufficiently healed for us to be oblivious of the original hurts which, although covered over, may still deeply affect the way we relate to the world around us.

How do we discover the scars that remain, and how do we continue the healing process? How do we reconnect and integrate all the parts of ourselves that we need in order to be whole and to develop to the full our own capacity to love and receive love, always remembering that this is a journey where it is more important to travel hopefully than to arrive.

The first step is to develop an awareness of the relationship we have with ourselves and others. We need to be able to accept ourselves, to give ourselves the kind of acceptance that we received, or would have liked to receive, from loving parents. Accepting ourselves as we are does not mean resigning ourselves to making the best of a bad job. Nor does it mean escaping from the responsibility of ourselves. Think again of the small baby who must be accepted just as it is. The challenge is to accept that at core you are perfect, not because of something you have done, or not done, but because you are unique. There is absolutely only one of you in the universe and therefore no one with whom to compare yourself. Your only task is to be as fully yourself as you can manage to be: to bring to fruition the potentiality that is you.

Certain problems may arise as you try to do this or even think about doing it. You might like to stop for a moment and consider the level of your own acceptance of yourself. Do you have any discomfort with the idea? You may even think the whole idea is rubbish.

The first problem is that it may seem presumptuous, even wicked, to consider yourself perfect. It is important here to be clear that not only are you essentially perfect, but that so is everyone else. Dr Stanislav Grof once defined the difference between a mystic and a psychotic person as follows. The mystic says: 'I am God', meaning God immanent in me – and in everyone else, the psychotic says 'I am God' meaning, me, alone. (Personal recollection from a workshop given by Dr Grof in Ireland, 1980.)

Accepting oneself as perfect does not mean thinking that there is no room for improvement. Paradoxically, by fully accepting yourself, you have the potential to free yourself from all the strivings to become something you are not and begin instead to nourish and support the person you can best become – yourself. Genuine acceptance of yourself with all of what you regard as strengths and weaknesses means saying in all humility and with complete compassion: 'This is me, and I am OK.' Not necessarily the biggest, the best, the brightest, the funniest, the anything'est, just myself, unique.

You may fear the risk of narcissistic self-absorption. This means having such an inflated ego – an inflated sense of oneself – that one is absorbed with the wonder of oneself. A consequence of poor self-esteem and feeling bad about ourselves is that we find various ways of defending ourselves from feeling so inadequate. For instance, we consciously keep ourselves down and find it hard to praise ourselves. Another way of coping is never to question yourself at all: to assume that you are great and that whenever something threatens it must be because of problems other people have. This kind of inflated ego does not come from deep appreciation and acceptance of yourself. Rather it comes from the fear of being anything less than great because if we admitted this to ourselves it would confirm our underlying sense of how disastrous we really are.

Difficulties with genuine self-acceptance arise from the many different ways we consider ourselves inadequate: less than competent, less than beautiful, less than intelligent – or whatever our aspirations are. It is so easy from all the messages we receive from early childhood on to believe that if only we could be different in some way we would then become acceptable – to whom it is seldom clear, but initially, to our parents and other role models. Then we frequently project all these expectations on to our image of God.

In fact the sense of guilt engendered by this process or by particular life experiences also becomes a major determinant in ensuring our inability to accept ourselves. Just as fear has the positive side of preventing us from going too far into danger, so guilt can indicate to us that we are moving away from integrity in some way. But when guilt increases and overwhelms us, we lose ourselves. Somehow we have to survive feeling that bad, so we cut off from the experience, losing the ability to listen to the subtle promptings that might have reached us were the system not overloaded.

The quantity of guilt we carry is not usually in proportion to the seriousness of the crimes we think we have committed. In fact people capable of committing serious crimes against others, (except in moments of desperation and overload) have usually cut off from their ability to feel much, if any, guilt. Conscience is a programme (like a computer program) that is created by what we learn at home and in the communities in which we live – both by what is said and by all the implicit messages that pass among the people around us. A child overwhelmed by parents with very high expectations may have such a finely tuned conscience that, unable to meet its demands no matter how hard he tries, may succumb to an obsessional illness. In this the terror is encapsulated and the whole psychological system finds it easier to become paralysed by focusing on some ritual like constant washing to ensure cleanliness than to face the horrors of disproportionate guilt that ordinary living would produce. So while our ability to feel guilty has a value, it can also have the opposite effect, making us feel so bad about ourselves that we no longer know who we are.

While total self-acceptance is proposed here as a step towards wholeness or individuation, it is also, in a way, a utopian concept. Had we come that far we would have reached or almost reached that place of wholeness itself. It is not therefore another aspiration to perfection to add to our list and then beat ourselves for not attaining. The task is more to develop an attitude of self-acceptance and compassion for oneself. The words of 'Desiderata', that poem variously attributed to Max Ebelman or a graveyard tombstone, are revealing:

Be gentle with yourself, for you too are a child
of the universe.

In practical terms, how can we work to recover ourselves and return to the source of our wellbeing – our love connection with the universe?

Many people undertake some stages of this journey through psychotherapy. The presence of another person as a guide and a reflector of what emerges is helpful, maybe even crucial at times. However, the essential ingredient is integrity and one's own willingness to be honest, challenging and compassionate with oneself.

One of the ways we can begin to recover ourselves, is simply by noticing the kind of self-talk we engage in. Most of the time we are talking to ourselves in different ways. We berate ourselves for not doing better; for not looking better or whatever; we tell ourselves how badly people are behaving; or we talk ourselves into new ideas.

If we begin to pay attention to our own inner dialogues, we can add positive messages to ourselves to counteract the constant judgements – whether they be judgements of self or of others. When we are telling ourselves what we did wrong, we can add something we did well. If we can't find something positive, we work at it until we can. Otherwise we're just rerunning an old tape which focuses on fault and does not know how to encourage, reward or support. If you're used to negative self-talk, positive self-talk can feel dishonest. It does not have to be. If you find that is the case, it is time to take stock. Studies of human behaviour demonstrate that behaviour is more effectively changed by rewarding behaviour you want to reinforce than by punishing behaviour you don't want.

We can learn to encourage ourselves by appreciating even the smallest things we do well. It is so easy to take good things for granted and focus on what goes wrong. This undermines what one would like to have happen. We need to learn to pay attention to our accomplishments, however meagre they may appear, appreciate ourselves for them and thereby reward and support the kind of behaviour we want to encourage in ourselves. Children respond best to attention. Too often they receive negative attention, that is, we put off giving them our full attention until they grab it by doing something we have to prevent, so their 'bad' behaviour gets our attention. So often, bad behaviour is reinforced in this way. It is important, of course, to impose limits, but if poor behaviour is the only way our children can get attention, then the incidence of that kind of behaviour will increase. Parents learn over and over again that even a short time spent playing with their child or listening to them with undivided attention will prevent many difficult hours of conflict and unhappiness.

We are all children at heart. It is worth remembering that and acknowledging that the child part of yourself needs your attention and support too. This child part is closest to the core self from which we often most want to distance ourselves, and we may refuse to acknowledge its existence. Yet this part of ourselves offers a gateway to the soul.

> I tell you this: unless you turn and become like children, you will never enter the Kingdom of Heaven. (Matthew 18: 2)

It is difficult to acknowledge the child within ourselves because we have spent so long learning to become adults. Adult behaviour is rewarded; childish behaviour is seen as simply that – childish, and unsuitable for adults. So we don't want to know about a possibly needy child within us.

We do need to become adults and behave in an adult fashion. In the process we often leave our inner child behind. The child does not mature quickly enough, perhaps because of insufficient nurturing, so we learn to fake it. Behaving as adults and discovering that such behaviour gets accepted and honoured, we begin to identify more with this adult self so that having acted 'as if' we were fully adult we eventually become adult. But as adults we need to be able to recover and nurture the child left behind if we are to enable this child to mature.

As the inner child grows stronger, the need to 'act' adult diminishes and a greater possibility emerges of relinquishing the role of adult and allowing the more complete person to emerge. This naturally matured child, now a more whole adult, is more likely to have retained the ability to be childlike, as distinct from childish, as part of its repertoire of ways of being in the world. The childlike quality is critical for our connection with soul, for it is open to wonder and awe, spontaneity and simplicity.

So how do we learn to acknowledge and nurture the child within? The answer to this question will be different for each of us. We begin by being gentle and supportive of ourselves as we are in the present. We can listen out for, or observe, ways in which our 'child' either looks for attention or avoids attention. This will probably be most evident in relations with others: when we seem to want more attention from others than they are willing to give; or we are quick to feel unloved and uncared for.

These are difficult areas to judge because other people too are dealing with the needs of their inner child selves.

Sometimes their refusal to acknowledge the needs within themselves shuts them off from their feelings so that, unable to handle closeness or intimacy and the feelings they would engender in them, they blame others for their neediness. So those close to us can say we demand too much of them when they are avoiding something in themselves, as well as when they have genuinely given of themselves and feel they are being called on to become a caretaker for needs of ours which go beyond the ability they could reasonably be expected to have to meet them.

Much of what we don't want to know about ourselves belongs to this child within, either because we have worked so hard to outgrow childhood or because of the ways in which the child was denigrated or hurt while we were still children. Children brought up in families where there is frequent disruption and friction do not live in a safe environment. It becomes necessary for them to control and hide themselves very early on in life. Fear dominates, and often shame. We feel shame as children when our parents do not behave as we think they should or when they say we are not behaving as we should. If our family appears to be the odd one out, we actually protect parents and siblings, often by covering up for them or trying to make things look better than they are, to teachers at school and other outsiders. Both in this case and in situations where they have suffered verbal, physical or sexual abuse (which of course is also physical), children feel somehow to blame, as if they were responsible for the problems – as in fact they are often accused of being.

The shame involved goes deep. In this instance opening up to the child within also means touching into these desperately uncomfortable feelings of shame. In fact to the adult self it can seem as if it is the child that the adult is ashamed of. It is therefore extremely hard to acknow-ledge the possible existence of such an internal child in the first place, let alone give it the kind of attention that means allowing oneself to feel the shame, fear and hurt that remain in the child. When one does so one has the experience of feeling ashamed of oneself: distinctions between child and adult self, already arbitrary, blur and it seems there is only one self, of which one is ashamed.

It is often the unacknowledged child within that influences our behaviour to a greater extent even than the adult self who appears to be in charge. Unknowingly protecting ourselves from the feelings of the child, we avoid situations which would touch into those feelings. This can affect our perceptions of others. Needing to keep them in their place so that their success doesn't threaten our own self-esteem, we can minimise their achievements and focus on their weak points, thereby enabling ourselves to feel bigger and more virtuous than we otherwise would.

Alternatively we may become peacemakers: agreeing to anything for peace; seeing others as right at all times; not valuing our own opinions and contributions. A further development of this experience can be a place of martyr-dom, where self-worth becomes based on the ability to placate and pacify people. Unwittingly you begin to value yourself for holding the moral high ground: the other person is nasty and demanding while you are peacemaking and pacifying and badly treated but can feel strong in being virtuous. The consequence of this pattern of behaviour is that one has a lot to lose if one begins to stand up for oneself and value one's innate worth instead of always yielding to others. It also prevents you from stopping others from treating you badly and allows them to get away with bad behaviour (which is also bad for them) and increases their inner feeling of guilt and poor self-esteem. So the vicious cycle of poor relationships continues.

If we are to ground ourselves more fully in love, then we have to heal our relationships. To do so we constantly have to interrupt the cycle of alienation from self by challenging ourselves and others with the vision of better possibilities. One way of doing this is by improving the way we communicate with one another. We will look further at this in Chapter 6.

Continuing to develop an awareness of the child within leads us to a greater sense of what its needs are and how we can best nurture and develop this core part of ourselves. A good way to continue is to find ways to dialogue with this internal self.

One possibility is to dialogue in writing. Another is to use one's imagination to picture the child within and to dialogue internally. You can write to the child, then write the response that you imagine the child is giving and then respond as the adult, and so on.

Similarly, you can dialogue internally by speaking to the child, having first pictured him/her as clearly as possible in your mind. You can ask the child what it has to say and then allow whatever comes to mind as a possibility to stand. The child may communicate more in a non-verbal than in a verbal way, so that needs to be given attention also.

In any one session, only a certain amount can happen. In fact, one would probably just introduce adult and child self initially. This form of dialoguing takes many sessions to develop and bear fruit so it is necessary to persevere.

There is no need to get caught up in worrying about whether something is 'just your imagination'. After all, it is one's own imagination and it needs to be recognised that out of all the myriad possibilities whatever has come is unique to you. So it is worth trusting and allowing oneself to go where your imagination takes you. If it feels all wrong, then this serious doubt can be included in your dialogue, both sides being allowed to discuss the dilemma. Children are often good at using their imagination, so the child may have some very pertinent things to say in this regard.

Finally, with the child's agreement, it is often useful to offer it some further nourishment and care. One can picture the child bathed in white light, or surrounded by sunlight, or you might hold the child in imagination, promising to take more care while holding him or her closely to you. Time needs to be allowed for the emotions which can sometimes arise when one does this. It is important to remember that emotions, most obviously tears but also anger, rage, fear and joy, bring great healing when allowed and acknowledged.

3

GROWING IN LOVE

The first thing many of us associate with love is the romantic thought of being 'in love'. The experience of being in love with someone who is also clearly in love with you has got to be one of the great joys of life. There is often pain intertwined with ecstasy, yet it is almost part of the whole experience: the pain of not being free to be together all the time or perhaps having to be parted for long periods: the contained passion that is an essential part of the pleasure of sexual fulfilment when it need be contained no longer.

Often opposites are only opposite sides of the one coin. Part of the joy of being in love is the pain of longing and wanting to be with someone else so much. Yet we would not want to forego the excitement and pleasure of being in love for the sake of avoiding the pain that comes with it, and that gives it an added tinge of excitement.

This image or experience of love is so powerful that it influences a huge proportion of our day-to-day lives. The commercial world knows its influence and much of what we buy, think and do is influenced by advertisements and marketing strategies that play on its importance. Candle-lit dinners with moonlight and soothing music evoke an expectation of intimacy and sensual experience that strikes a chord deep within. Whether we have not yet known what it is to be in love or we look back with nostalgic memories, such images evoke strong currents of feeling.

Underneath the romantic images, the sexual pulse beats like a drum in a tribal ritual. Its compelling rhythm is part of every nuance of the relationship – so much a part that it blinds us to the other aspects of love which may become all important later on. However, the sexual element is also the vital energy – the spice that gives life to the whole experience and without which the rest would not exist.

Although many attempts are made to separate sexual and romantic love, to separate body and heart, is in fact impossible to do so if one is really in the throes of the experience of being in love. Despite all attempts to deny it, sexuality is part of this experience of loving and it is genuinely not possible here to separate body from head and from heart. This is true of all of life. Body, heart and mind, feelings, thinking and soul are intrinsically linked, but in all other areas it is easier to deny this reality. When we are in love, body and heart and soul are undeniably present.

Ideally, the sexual expression of such a love should be the fusion of body, mind and spirit. In surrendering to their love and passion and to each other, the couple could meet not only through the heart and the body, but also on the level of their souls, so that their experience would be one not only of human love but also of union with the divine. This is the archetypal image that is encapsulated in many wedding liturgies and theologies but it is probably a rare experience. Few of us have the depth of experience of self and other that would open us to this level of union. Still, the union of a couple deeply in love has the great potential of also bringing them closer to an awareness of their spirituality by offering them a glimpse of what it would be to be in union with their own souls – their connection with that which is both themselves and something far greater.

Sexuality and spirituality – so often polarised – should not be separated. To be fully human means to be fully all that we are. We are sensual and sexual beings. To the extent that we are less than fully human, we are also less than fully divine. Cut off from ourselves, we are cut off from God. As we recover the parts we have lost, we become less alienated from who we really are and as we do so, we discover ourselves as an embodied expression of God, or Love, living on this planet at the present moment in time.

Many images come to mind when one begins to think about marriage and they are not all necessarily loving pictures. The first thing one can say is that marriage presents one with a challenge. The challenge is to create a lasting love partnership that will continue to enrich the lives of the partners after the first bloom of romance has faded.

This journey begins with a commitment. So there is an intention of will expressed and a decision made. In the long term this partnership agreement and the couple's experience of having journeyed together will become the container for the relationship. Within this container individual needs and attitudes may shift and change and it is hoped the relationship will be strong enough to allow for varying degrees of movement within it.

If the marriage is to be growth-enhancing, it will have to allow for both partners to be dependent on one another and also for each to be independent and to follow their own star. The shared experience of life and of support for one another can lead to a mature love, deep and satisfying in ways that may be quite different from initial romantic engagement. So the image of mature love is mellow and warm, closer to the nectar of ripe fruit or a mature wine than the fizz and excitement of a lemon sorbet or champagne which one might associate with early romance. This is a love that is savoured and appreciated and that takes a long time to mature. The road is long with many twists and turns and a successful partnership depends on the commitment of both parties although one or other partner may hold the commitment, almost alone, for periods of time.

Marriage then shows us love as a process that develops, deepens and changes over time. A commitment to be present for the process is needed and the process itself will be one in which the relationship is transformed and also plays its part in the transformation of the partners concerned.

Family life – intrinsically linked with love – is the most fundamental crucible we experience. Throughout our lives our experience of family will nourish, challenge and sustain us in love and in ability to love. The love we experience as a baby, child and adult and the way that love is expressed will be crucial for our development and deeply affect the way we experience romance and choose, or don't choose, adult partners for ourselves. It will also affect the way we relate to the spiritual force which we in the West, mostly, call God.

The challenge of parenting, if it becomes part of our lives, will probably teach us more about the complexities of the issues involved in expressing love than any other experience. We will be called upon to love with deep feeling, in very practical ways, to give and to take, to hold and to let go and all of these experiences will add to and change the people we are ourselves.

Looking at the progression of family life, we observe both how the child is shaped to love and how parents are challenged to develop their ability to love. Parents love their children from birth to the grave. Where there are exceptions to this, they come from an experience of great hurt. The love may not always be obvious to both parties – misunderstandings, hurt and estrangements may be frequent – but behind it all, parents, in the vast majority of cases, matter to their children and children are important to their parents for life.

Parents meet the basic physical needs of the child for survival by providing it with food and shelter and physical contact. In fact nurturance is an essential ingredient in what we call love. Whether or not they made a deliberate choice to conceive a baby, they are committed to caring for it. The utter helplessness of the child and its dependence on them demands their commitment to nurture it until it can survive and thrive on its own.

In most instances, this commitment is taken for granted and parents begin the task of nurturing the growth of this new person. In the process, much will be learned. Their commitment will demand a lot from them and reward them greatly. They will sacrifice sleep, time, social events, money and the things they could have spent it on in order to love their child to the best of their ability. Most of the time this will not be experienced as a sacrifice because, although these are indeed real losses, the rewards of being with their own children and seeing them develop and grow and the reward of the bond itself will far outweigh any apparent sacrifices.

Their commitment will be an expression of their love. In the first years they will offer gentle acts of encouragement: comforting the hurt child when it cuts its knee or cuddling the fractious toddler until it falls asleep. So gentleness, comfort, warmth and cuddles provide us with images of a particular kind of loving. The deep feelings for the child that well up also tell us something of what it means to love.

These everyday experiences are familiar to us and we can take them for granted. However, such experiences help us to ground our vision of love. Love is sublime, may be divine, yet it is also everyday acts of kindness. Our relationship to love affects all our everyday actions and decisions.

As the child begins to grow, the parents' love will express itself in a new and less obvious way. The child will need to have limits imposed. Parents will say 'no' to certain behaviour and insist on others: 'no' to actions that can lead to danger: 'no' to constant demands to have things exactly how the toddler wants them. The loving parent now has to learn to balance too many limits with too much freedom. The child will experience the frustration of limits but also the security that comes from living in a world that is manageable. Too wide a space, too much freedom and the child will experience the world as too large and frightening.

If you observe a toddler with its mother in a new place, you will notice that the child will explore the space but frequently return to her mother. If she is too frightened she won't move away from her mother at all. The security that comes from the limits parents impose is not only because the child is contained within a safe space but also because as she moves out into the world and grows bigger she is reassured to come up against the caring of her parents and to discover that they are still in charge and she is not alone in this big expanse of which she has had little experience. Hence she is not overwhelmed by fear and can continue to feel confident in her explorations. As she grows older, the wise parent allows the limit to be constantly moved back, providing an ever wider expanse of world for her to take the risk to explore and to learn from. This happens geographically: from house to garden to neighbourhood to taking bus journeys alone to travelling the world. It also happens psychologically in terms of learning to know how to handle more and more of life's experiences, until, as an adult, she can explore alone.

In this way she also becomes secure enough to be able, later, to trust the world enough to take the risk of loving others. Loving others involves an investment, a step of faith, which can only be taken from secure ground.

For many people, their explorations end when they reach adulthood. Adults impose their own limits on the territory – both geographical and experiential – that they are willing to explore, thus keeping their world manageable and giving themselves at least the illusion of security. Further exploration seems unnecessary to many people and takes place only when life throws something at them that can be dealt with by no other means than by extending the boundaries of their experience.

The journey to love, however, is a journey that calls us to continue with our development in adult life. This process requires us to be willing to explore the limits we now impose upon ourselves – limits of knowledge, attitudes, experiences, and places we'll visit. It is tempting to close our minds and easy to define ourselves as people who believe in certain things, behave in certain ways, who have a particular way of living and who expect, usually, to remain within certain defined geographical territory.

Continuing our journey in adult life requires opening our hearts and minds to possibilities that can teach us new things and bring us to new places both within ourselves and in the world.

Coming back to parenting and what it can show us about love, we see in it a sense of connection, nurturance, security and encouragement to grow. Parents offer something else which has a direct bearing on the child's, and later the adult's, relationship to his or her self. They offer, at best, an appreciation and unconditional acceptance of the child which has far-reaching effects on the child's sense of self-worth and value.

Parents appreciate their children, and children are helped by this experience to feel sure of their place and value in the world. This appreciation from their parents and others helps them ultimately to appreciate and value themselves and hence to maintain the sense of themselves that will be so important in their future development.

Parental love also has the potential to offer a deep acceptance of the child simply because of the connection between them. This is the kind of love that continues to love even when the more superficial layers of the relationship have broken down. So that even when there are severe difficulties in the relationship and it may appear to have irretrievably broken down, there is still a connection of love. It may even be just because the love is so great that the potential hurt can be so great, causing people to break away from each other even when the bond remains.

When the child grows beyond the need for parental nurturance and reaches adulthood, the loving parent faces a new challenge. Is their love large enough to enable them to let go? In loving another, many of our needs are met. Even our own self-esteem can be based on the love and care we give to others. When it is time for the young adult to leave the nest parents are faced not only with losing the constant presence of the young person in their lives, but with needs of their own, the existence of which they may not even have realised. In caring for the young person these needs were met, but now the time has come to face parts of themselves that were unknown and to meet needs in new ways. If one has 'rules' that say that adults should not or do not have needs, then it can be doubly daunting to discover such needs in oneself.

Apart altogether from the aspects of self that come to the surface when a young person moves out of home , there is a real loss involved which needs to be acknowledged.

There may be relief and a welcome sense of freedom from responsibilities that have been around for a long time but there is very frequently grief: grief that people whom you love as much, or more, than anyone else in the world are moving away. You do not know what the future will hold for you without them.

It has been said that until you let something go you never know whether you had it in the first place. Loving parents are challenged to let their children go and still remain open to them. This means not closing off the pain but allowing oneself to be both sad and happy at the same time – sad at the loss of separation and glad that a job has been well done and that the young person is now adult enough to go out into the world and take responsibility for themselves.

Remaining open means being available to listen, support and encourage – and even sometimes to advise as it is requested, but also being able to cope with not necessarily being asked to do any of these. Time to get on with our own lives.

This letting go is one of the many times in life we are challenged to learn to surrender something that is precious to us. There is grief involved but also the opportunity to learn that we are not dependent on those we love. We can love and we can let go and we can love again.

The process opens the opportunity to learn of the love within us upon which we can always depend.

We have looked briefly in this chapter at several aspects of love that present themselves in day to day life and will take a further look at the implications of these in future chapters. These experiences are the crucibles of everyday life, out of which our capacity for love and our ability to deliver it grow.

A further aspect of love needs to be mentioned here. Often when we think of love we think of altruistic love: actions of courage and expressions of care and concern that overcome mountains of difficulties to relieve pain and suffering. These images seem to encapsulate the essence of love and its transforming power. They inspire and remind one of much more human potential for greatness than seems obvious in day to day living.

Many images come to mind: work being done in Romanian orphanages; Bob Geldof's Live Aid concert; volunteers working in African refugee centres and the face of Mother Theresa of Calcutta. The face of the last is particularly striking. This is so because, at a time when religious orders have had minimal numbers coming forward with vocations, many flocked to join Mother Theresa. In some way, through the images of Malcolm Muggeridge who wrote about her, she personified love in such a way that it inspired large numbers of people. It seems that when we see such love in action it calls forth something in us that transcends self and seems worth great sacrifice to attain. There is an element of faith in such love and an unwillingness to let anything get in the way of just loving. There is something about loving that has a quality of truth to it that is almost irresistible to us.

It will be seen, from the glimpses we have had, that there are many facets to human loving. Love is a word that covers a multitude of human experiences which have something in common. This book is about our relationship with love. It is about our need to be loved, about loving ways and about our need to love. It will also suggest that love itself may be central to who we are and that our life's journey is a crucible - transmuting us in love.

4

LOVE AS A DEVELOPMENT PROCESS

Life is a process of development. From birth, through learning to crawl, to walk and talk, the process is easily discernible. One stage follows fast on another and the child, literally, grows in front of our eyes.

The child learns from what it is taught but it also carries within it an organic tendency to develop and grow. This growth process can be nurtured or stunted by the environment in which the child lives, but unless it is severely undernourished in multiple ways or suffers an accident or major illness, the child will grow to adulthood. The adult will continue to mature through life. Continued ageing is an organic process which continues one way or another, regardless of what we want.

In one sense, perhaps it is possible to describe life as a process of becoming, of moving further towards a tendency to love. Just as there is a physical process which goes on unfolding - carrying us on to the next stage of physical development - so there seems to be potential for the development of the rest of one's being.

Whatever we are in life, or at whichever moment, we are also in the process of becoming something else. Just as we finish one thing (or maybe even before), something else takes our attention and we move on to give our attention to that.

Often we believe that life is static and expect it to continue on in much the same way. Or we feel that if it does change, it should do so because of choices we've made: for example, to move house or change job. If life changes we expect the external things to alter. However, we also change and develop internally. If we stay attuned to our inner process we may have a sense of an ongoing internal development process that we can either nurture and follow or tune out of and ignore.

It is not usually part of western culture to bring this process to our attention. Things that are known by intuition, feeling, images or experience are not highly rated in a culture that has emphasised the role of the intellect to the extent that often only scientific and academic knowing is acknowledged as knowledge at all. Yet we know many things without having any scientific or analytic understanding of them. We know how to walk, breathe, talk, relate to others, sing, make love, pray, dance – the list is endless – without normally having any idea in theory of how we do such things. People were competent in all these areas before we had anything remotely related to the present scientific paradigm (the particular model of the world currently used in science). The internal development process is something to which we do consciously have to attune ourselves and if we are to follow this path to developing our potential (that is to become the selves we potentially are) then we must also respond appropriately to what we 'hear'.

More will be said about learning to listen and respond

to this internal growth process later on. For now, what is important is the understanding that life is not static. Just because things are as they are right now, there is no reason to assume that this is how they will continue for ever. At times it might be comforting to imagine that they could always remain the same, but it is very helpful to remind oneself that feelings do not stay the same. So the grief one feels today will not be the grief of tomorrow and the joy of today will be qualitatively different in the future.

This is important to be clear about because so often we assume that the way we are now is the way we will be for ever.

It has been suggested that there are stages in adult development. The first is about becoming an adult in the way that is generally understood: to develop a strong ego self, a sense of knowing who you are and the ability to be clear about the roles you adopt in life. What is required at this stage of life is an ability to fit in and be well adjusted. Most of the time we are judged by society on our apparent success in participating in society in this way and by the way we comply competently with the major norms (generally expected behaviour) of the society in question.

This stage of ego development is described by Susan Jeffares as the stage of 'becoming somebody' (in *Dare to Connect*, 1992). We know who we are then if we can reply to the question 'who am I?': with answers such as 'I am 28 years old'; 'I am a nurse'; 'I like classical music'; 'I drive a Volkswagen Golf'; 'I vote Labour' or with other factual information about the way we live and the things we believe in.

During the next stage the focus changes and is more on the need to be authentic than the need to be well adjusted. John Rowan makes a very important point about this and future stages in his book, *The Transpersonal*. Up to this stage, society encourages and endorses development, but from here on one is on one's own. This stage is counter-cultural in particular ways. Seeking authenticity means exploring the boundaries of cultural norms. What one has taken for granted as the valid norms and values of life one now has to question in a new way. Carl Rogers, a psychologist and pioneer counsellor, was asked in an interview on RTE television ('Personally Speaking', 1985) about the application of his research findings on education. The research suggests that people would be better educated if facilitated to learn rather than by the 'cup and jug' method of filling people up with information. He replied that he had regretfully come to the conclusion that his findings would not be implemented because they are too threatening. Too much is invested in maintaining the status quo.

When people are genuinely supported in their efforts to think for themselves in an authentic way, they will challenge things that are taken for granted. If Rogers is correct then this has serious implications for society at large. While education apparently values the ability to think clearly for oneself, in fact this ability may be valued only within prescribed limits. Mass movements such as the rise of Naziism in Germany earlier this century may perhaps be partly understood in this context. We cannot have it both ways. If people are to learn to think things through for themselves they will not always uphold the status quo. If they do not think like this they will have a greater tendency towards compliance and acceptance than towards authenticity. When charismatic public figures speak authoritatively the people who have always respected authority will tend to respect and follow their leadership – whether for good or bad.

There are also those who habitually rebel against authority and this is, of course, another dependency trap. Sometimes those who rebel use the idea of authenticity to justify their rebellions but the search for authentic action means searching for the truth (in so far as one can discern it) in any particular moment or situation and it is necessary to move beyond one's characteristic dependency patterns – whether that is a pattern to conform or to rebel.

This is an oversimplified description of the dangers of a society in which the norms and values of society are presented as true morality and people are not taught ways of seeking truth and evaluating the rights and wrongs of a situation and the importance of being true to themselves. In practice we are usually motivated by a more complex mixture of the desire to follow the truth and the desire to be accepted by our society.

Moving towards authenticity means seeking to know who we are. In seeking to be true to ourselves we are continually challenged to find out who that self really is. It requires a focus inwards. In trying to express who we are, we discover gaps, or questions arise about the way we react or feel in certain situations that need to be explored further. The search for the truth of oneself is, again, often a journey that is taken with the facilitation of a psychotherapist. As we learn to acknowledge and follow our feelings we discover how emotions are located in the body. When we tune into our bodies, we discover that the body can have a wisdom all of its own. This stage in the process of our development will be the time when we particularly realise that body and person are one.

Whether these stages follow straightforwardly one after another or whether development is more like a spiral that brings us to consider the same issues at different depths of our being as we go around it, there is an internal process at work that we need to discover and then facilitate. The process usually challenges us to discover the place in our lives where we have been hurt or injured and the defensive patterns we have established to enable us to deal with life. We follow a process of healing in order to recover the parts of ourselves that were lost. It seems that as we move forward, we are called to explore the past more deeply– or the difficulties of the past, especially the unresolved dilemmas as they present themselves in the present time for resolution. This healing process – a journey towards wholeness, or completion – is a lifelong journey which requires different things of us at different times.

Many of us want to start at a different place from where we are, maybe because we don't know where we are, or because we are loathe to take the time to find out or because we want to be spiritual high flyers. Or we want to be more advanced than where the mundane issues of our current lives place us.

David Whyte, a poet whose whole way of speaking and presenting his poetry is like a dance, once said: 'When you are lost in the wood, stop and listen . . . take a look around

. . . the tree beside you is not lost'. ('Close to Home, Zoological Imagination', Lecture, 1994.) We are often in such a hurry to get somewhere that we have no idea where we are. Always the first step is to discover where we are. The way unfolds one step at a time. The critical – maybe the only question – is: are we on the path?

Having learned to take more responsibility for ourselves and our own healing process and recovered our identification with our bodies and thus our separateness one from another, the next stage might bring us on to an awareness of the ways in which we are separate yet also connected.

This is the level where we dip into the collective unconscious. It was Carl Jung who first outlined the notion of a collective unconscious, suggesting that as well as our conscious selves and our unconscious selves (the part of our personal psyche of which we are unaware) we also have access to the collective unconscious. This has also been described as racial memory. It is the realm of symbols that are deeply significant to us because they touch into a part of the psyche that is common to us all. While we each have individual childhood experiences and no one's experience is the same as anybody else's, on the level of the collective unconscious, we know things that relate to experiences that are also true for others. It is suggested that many of the truths portrayed in myths and legends are of this order. The hero archetype is one to which we all relate, not just as the hero of one particular story but as the hero in many stories.

It is because of our strong connection to these archetypal images that myths hold such truth. Sometimes there is more truth conveyed in myth than there would be if the events portrayed took place in ordinary everyday reality. This is where confusion and conflict can arise in discussing religious truths. For some, it is crucial that the events written about in the Bible or other religious books of truth took place historically as described. But the truth of such stories can be greater when acknowledged on the level of myth because myth has a quality that touches the depths of the individual psyche in ways that chronicalised events do not. It is somewhat similar to the way in which poetry can say something to us which a matter-of-fact prose description of the same event or emotion would not.

At one stage in his journeys, Christ spoke to the Pharisees – the upholders of law and order – asking whether it was more important to heal the sick or not to work on the Sabbath. In this, and so many ways, he challenged his followers and detractors to look at the spirit of truth, not the letter of the law, and to act out of the spirit of love rather than out of the rule of law. He made it clear that the law is important, that we do need structures in our lives, but the spirit of love is greater – the process of life itself is greater than the container. It is the wine that is important, not the chalice that contains it.

On the level of the collective unconscious, it is possible for us to connect with one another in a way that goes beyond speech, through the senses and through imagery.

Rather than identifying ourselves totally as embodied selves, on this level we begin to identify ourselves as a centre of pure consciousness. 'I' am defined by the Other or Others. This is how John Rowan describes it in *The Transpersonal*. In other words, who we are is defined, we sense, more by the divine that is beyond ourselves (whether within the depths of self or external to ourselves) than by our physical embodied self.

This is not to deny the truth of our previous understanding of ourselves but simply to suggest that we are even more than we previously realised and that some aspects of the way we understood ourselves before are now redundant and can be shed much as a snake sheds its skin when it has grown out of it.

Through deep imagery and intuition we feel ourselves to be in touch with something beyond ourselves and greater than ourselves, but which is also part of ourselves. This is the level at which we may be 'guided' by many entities. Here 'God' speaks to us through many forms and images. Such archetypal images (as we described them earlier) may come as figures from myths and stories the patterns of which recur in different forms. We may be led by angels or animals or spirit guides which speak to us in numinous ways, or we may be led by the gods of myth, such as gods and goddesses of ancient times. Such images may also present themselves in a way that is more relevant to previous stages of our development, where they represent sub-personalities or parts of the self that need to be acknowledged and heard.

In working with such images, we do not always have to know on what level we are operating, so long as we treat them with respect and neither deify nor regard them as anything greater or lesser than messages to which we need to listen and with which we need to dialogue so as to achieve further understanding and direction for our life's journey.

It is suggested that in the next stage of our journey we would transcend such images. It seems that we might then identify ourselves more as pure spirit. This experience of self has been described as 'neither this nor that', a level at which 'I' is not defined, or is maybe beyond definition. This is the realm of the mystics – described by Taoism, Christian mysticism, Zen and the goddess mystics, to name but a few.

Drawing on the work of Ken Wilber, Rowan, who has been a guide through this map of the transpersonal, distinguishes between soul and spirit. He suggests that soul is that with which we identify on the subtle level – where we have talked of the collective unconscious – and that spirit is what we relate to at the more advanced, causal, level of the mystics. Perhaps soul is our connection with spirit, a more personal aspect of the spirit to which we may ultimately come to surrender ourselves as we identify ourselves as spirit.

These stages are briefly described to show how, in adult development, one can have a different sense of oneself at different stages. At any one time one does not have the final answer to one's true self but one can come closer to a more complete picture. The process of growth never ends, although as we become increasingly aware of it we may possibly become more identified with the process itself. At each stage the learning of the previous stage is integrated and transcended. So the previous learning is not redundant but a necessary part of the present situation.

We have not looked here at the stages of childhood development that precede the adult stages and of course people's development may be arrested at any stage. One of the difficulties in adulthood can be to separate experiences that relate to childhood needs from those that relate to stages further on. It is possible to confuse, for example, images from the subtle self or soul level with those which relate more to childhood issues. This is where guidance from a transpersonal psychotherapist or spiritual teachers can be helpful. However, if we are genuinely in touch with our own development and the unfolding process of our inner selves – and not trying to push ourselves to some-where we have not yet arrived – then there is less danger of such confusion arising.

The foregoing outline of a potential development process for each one of us is given as a map. It suggests that there is a territory to explore and urges us to go on exploring. There is something beyond the horizon, and we will not fall over the edge of the world if we dare to journey beyond what is familiar. When the journey takes us over the horizon of the last known territory, it can feel scary and uncomfortable but so long as we are genuinely connected to and following our inner wisdom and take one step at a time, the journey is worthwhile. In the Christian tradition this inner wisdom is promised to the followers of Christ in St John's Gospel 'I will leave you with a Counsellor . . . the Spirit of Truth.' (John 14:5)

In the famous phrase of Korzybski: 'A map is not the territory.' The map is only an indicator of the possibilities of the journey. It tells us very little about the actual territory each individual will cover, nor about how far it is appropriate for each of us to travel. It can be useful to know that the territory has been mapped, however roughly, and that there are markers available which can help us to think about the area in which we find ourselves.

The map which is being drawn on here has been outlined by Ken Wilber after intensive study of differing schools of psychology and the experiences of the mystical traditions of major world religions and relates to what he, after Aldous Huxley, calls the 'perennial wisdom'. This journey has recognisable stages regardless of the religious beliefs which guide and inform it. This is not to denigrate religion – quite the opposite. It seems that whichever route we take to climb, the mountain has signposts which will direct us to the top. Sometimes we find signposts more enlightening that derive from less familiar religions than that of our upbringing, perhaps because they have become less tarnished by familiarity and the way we looked at them at earlier stages in our lives. In this book, deliberate references are made to Christianity because it is culturally embedded in society in much of the Western world. However, the way it is presented, and our familiarity with it, has dulled our eyes to much of its deeper potential. Much of our church experience, with its emphasis on control, has also left us with a lot of distress, hurt and confusion about the message of love that Christ proclaimed.

It can be useful to recover our Christian roots, first of all because we often need to heal the wounds of bad experiences in order to recover an openness to love and secondly because this is the path of our culture and it can lead us to be more grounded in our way. Society needs religion and Christianity needs people following the path of transforming love and willing to share the spirit of truth as it is revealed today.

It seems important to remember the uniqueness of each individual journey. It would be false to assume that each individual has a journey to undertake that goes through particular stages and that if they do not reach a particular place in that journey, then in some way they have failed.

Journeys have been recorded that follow this pattern. That does not mean we must assume the same journey is appropriate for everyone.

The image of a tapestry demonstrates the importance of a multitude of threads, each taking their own path. For anyone to follow another's path, or present themselves in an alternative colour, would be to ruin the order of the whole picture. It is very easy to assume that because something is true or appropriate for one person, it must be right for all. People must fulfil their destiny in very different ways. The world needs artists and scientists, homemakers and soldiers, those who know how to nurse the ill and those who minister to the soul.

What is important is not where we are or where we're going to - it is whether we are on the path that is right for us and that will take us on the way that is appropriate for us to follow. This shows us the danger of evangelising and of judging the path of another because we do not know what their way is and have enough trouble in finding the way for ourselves. It is a lifelong task to remove 'the plank from (our) own eye(s)', as Jesus advised a disciple (Matthew 7: 5) , in order for us to see the path ahead just that little bit clearer.

5

OPENING THE HEART TO LOVE THROUGH GRIEF

Life is potentially a developmental process which we can ignore or assist. There is a way in which we can instinctively know what needs to happen to facilitate this process, but often we have cut ourselves off from this instinctive knowing because we do not realise it is there to access and/or because we have ceased to listen to its promptings.

Potentially, life can be seen as a process of becoming – starting with birth and moving towards completion. The journey to wholeness is a journey to become more fully what we are – at which stage we would be ready to transcend this life as we know it and death would naturally be the next stage or the boundary to cross to the next level of existence, whatever that would be.

This is an overview of the situation. Of more immediate concern are the ways in which we go about: healing the hurts that have been caused by various life experiences; dealing with the difficulties in our relationships that make them less than the loving experiences we might like them to be; and recovering from the loneliness and isolation that is part of our experience of alienation.

One of the ways in which we heal our hurt is by allowing ourselves to grieve. Most of what we have learned discourages us from doing this. Yet in many ways grief is an intrinsic part of everyday life. Every time we move on in life – whether it be from school, from college or work or from one house to another – we leave something behind. In fact the ability to leave what was yesterday's behind and live in the present of today will be very important. Yet every time this movement forward takes place there is a loss involved. However pleased we may be to go forward, it is sad to leave behind the pleasures and familiarity of the past. The past is known territory and moving forward inevitably means some loss of security. Most of the time, because of our conditioning and because of the discomfort of it, we don't let ourselves feel the sadness. Many people have difficulty with good-byes. If pressed as to a reason for this they will often say 'I'd only cry' or 'I'm afraid I'd break down'.

This perceived need to hold oneself together and never break down has serious consequences. It is also, of course, a strength and a resource. There are situations where we do have to carry on and not break down, the most obvious being where emergency teams have to deal with horrific calamities and operate at peak efficiency. There are times when we need to be able to defend ourselves and to close our inner selves off and contain ourselves so that we can be present to others in particular ways. It is when that pattern becomes so rigid that we can never let ourselves feel the pain or the shock that we have gone too far. Many, many losses, especially small ones, can be accumulated without trouble. Then when we might wish to feel the sadness of a particular parting we may be afraid to do so because of the backlog of feelings.

Where serious losses have taken place, such as the death of people one has loved, and active grieving has not followed, then in another loss situation, one can be afraid to cry for fear that the floodgates will open. People often say this: 'I was afraid the floodgates would open and I'd never be able to stop or close them again.' This image is very appropriate. It is of a dam with all the tears piled up behind it and the fear that if the dam burst or the gates opened, the person would be destroyed by the ensuing flood. This is unlikely to be the case, but the fear is real nonetheless. In such a situation, it is seldom that people can actually open the floodgates sufficiently to let the grief flow so tumultuously. It is usually released only in a trickle, sometimes moving towards a flow. It can happen that their grief overwhelms them for a while and that they are unable to carry on with their usual duties, just as one would expect of someone after a serious bereavement.

The difficulty can be that the breakthrough may finally have come long after such a bereavement and it is then problematic to find an excuse for taking the space for this healing process. This is where our attitudes to loss need to change. Thankfully we are becoming much more aware of the importance of grief. There is less tendency – although still too much – to keep the immediately bereaved from crying, and bereavement counselling services help to spread the word that grief is healing and valuable. Many of us would still be inclined to seek medication from doctors to prevent the flow rather than ask for a sick certificate to enable us to go through an intensive healing bout of grief if that were what was needed.

Tears are genuinely part of natural healing. Very often

people will do anything to suppress this natural course and seek alternative 'healing' in the form of drugs to help them suppress it. It is, of course, the antithesis of healing and simply delays the healing process. This is a real problem for doctors. Many people decry the fact that doctors give out prescriptions so readily for unnecessary drugs. Doctors despair because of the unrealistic expectations with which people come to them. We have come to expect modern medicine to have a cure for every ill, including every miserable feeling. We do not expect to have uncomfortable feelings and assume that the doctor should be able to remove them.

General practitioners spend an enormous proportion of their time dealing with socio-medical problems: difficulties with relationships; housing difficulties; job worries and stress-related problems.

Part of the difficulty with facing into grief and allowing ourselves fully to experience the pain and the anger is the sense that it will go on for ever. This is why an awareness of life as an ongoing process, as discussed in the last chapter, is so important. This is true not only on the macro level, when taking an overall view of one's life, but also on the micro level. Day to day, we move through things. A small graze or cut goes through a healing process. There is bleeding (sometimes quite profuse) then quite quickly the cut begins to heal and goes through the stages of repair until there is only a small scar and then none at all. This healing process can be similar in situations where we feel emotional pain. Allowing ourselves to cry or show anger is part of the normal recovery process. The body and psyche know how to heal themselves and we can intervene too much, deciding we know better than nature. Over-control interferes with the natural healing process.

Having learned to control, we then fail to experience the natural healing that would teach us how it could be. Thus we no longer believe that it is safe to go through things, imagining that if we let them take their course, there will be no recovery. This is the way we delude ourselves. We think we need more ways to keep in control. When all our ability to keep the lid on things and keep control runs out, we then have to ask doctors for remedies to strengthen our control mechanisms. Instead of asking them to facilitate the healing process, we ask them to help us maintain and strengthen a maladaptive pattern that, encouraged by many social norms, we have established for ourselves in the first place.

There is an added difficulty at this stage. Because we are so used to keeping control and not allowing ourselves to feel emotions, it becomes additionally threatening to let the control go. There can now be the added experience of feeling as if you are losing oneself. You are not, but because you are so used to being one way in the world, that is in control, in losing that total sense of control, it can feel as if you are losing yourself. Of course in one way this is true. You are losing the person you were – the self who was always in control. This is where breaking down is really breaking through, both to one's real self and also to a more healthy way of functioning. The controlled self is the self-created persona that we present to the world for protection and in order to conform with the expectations of society. We come to identify so completely with this self that the more natural self who is behind the armour is lost.

In many ways, in the western world today, we are being challenged with the limits of over-control. We control our natural processes and delude ourselves that this is healthy; we control the environment around us and ignore the earth's natural processes. We put more and more chemicals on the earth to make it produce more, then have to try to revitalise dead land that has been so over-farmed it is open to all kinds of disease. We denude the earth of forests and its life-giving properties and are then constantly challenged with more and more things which need to be controlled. We have polluted rivers and there is now a growing hole in the ozone layer which threatens the very earth we depend on. Our control is so out of control that we are a great danger, both to our species and to the rest of the planet. We thought and still think we can make a better job of nature than nature. No doubt we humans do have resources that are our contribution to the planet. But we are too presumptuous and have such an inflated sense of our own importance that we do not trouble ourselves to see where those resources fit in. Instead we want to run everything, in a way that suits us. Greed has taken over. Such need for control stems from fear. Then we have to find ever more effective ways of warding off the secondary fear that perhaps we are not really, after all, in total control.

This starts at home for each of us. We are not totally in control of our lives. When we love we open ourselves. Opening ourselves we are vulnerable. Being vulnerable we are not in control. We are not managing everything to protect ourselves but allowing ourselves to care about others and to get involved. This involvement means that we are in relationship and to the extent that others will also meet us openly, we connect and make contact.

This kind of contact is the opposite of alienation. Being in relationship makes us less likely to actively hurt others and less willing to damage our immediate environment. Because we feel a loving connection we are sensitive and therefore open to the pain we feel ourselves if we hurt others. Their pain affects us. To prevent this, we have to harden our hearts and close down. This is something we do all the time to protect ourselves from the harshness around us, from our disappointments and from the pain of our grief.

Remembering our loss opens us to grief. Grieving, when it is intense, breaks the heart. When people suffer great loss they have either to freeze their hearts and try to turn them to stone or break their hearts open with grief. Such grieving is intensely painful. Yet when a heart breaks open it is transformed. A cold heart can always be melted if the person is willing to allow it be warmed. When the warmth is let in, when the person concerned makes some contact, however small, on a heart level – then the active grieving can begin to take place. As the tears flow, hearts open. When the heart is open the person concerned is open to love and to receiving love. In a small way tears of happiness demonstrate what is meant. When we are touched, whether by joy or pain, grief flows as part of the heart's grief is melted and released.

In the immediate reaction to a serious bereavement, it is not only because of the control we excercise over ourselves that our feelings are suppressed. In the first throes of loss we are so shocked and overwhelmed by grief that it is common to feel numbed and deadened. It is almost only after some time, even some considerable time like this that we may be sufficiently recovered from the immediate blow and sufficiently strong to be able to begin again the kind of active grieving process that has been described here.

Sometimes the blow is so great that it is as if there is nothing left of us. It has gone so deep that our normal defences do not work. The somebody self seems not to be there; the internal self, so wounded, seems numbed and we move more from a sense of automation than from any sense of self. This is the period, in particular, when medication may be appropriate, if only to help us protect ourselves sufficiently to get through. Many people want medication to avoid every pain, but there are others who are so afraid of medication that they have difficulty in accepting badly needed help.

When we love another, we open ourselves to the possibility of experiencing hurt. By letting someone matter enough to us that their absence can cause us pain, we make ourselves vulnerable. Vulnerability is part and parcel of loving. Unless we are willing to open ourselves in this way, we cannot love nor let in the love of another.

Having experienced the pain of loss or the hurt of rejection, very often we are loth to open ourselves to such a possibility again. But while we protect ourselves in this way we also remain closed to the possibilities of love – to the warmth, nurturance, intimacy and joy that love can bring. By controlling our tears and depressing our rage, we contain and depress ourselves, deadening ourselves to life and the possibilities of relationship.

Emotions are fluid and need to be processed by allowing them to flow. Freezing our emotions or hardening ourselves against feelings has the effect of turning a fluid process into something solid and hard which we then find hard to deal with.

This is not to suggest a constant acting out of emotions. Where people need to dramatise their emotions as distinct from simply allowing them to be, then something else is at work. Because we have become so insensitive to feeling at all, we sometimes find it hard to tell the difference. In recovering an ability to feel we become more sensitive and better able to distinguish between feelings that flow as part of the natural pulse of life and those that are expressed dramatically in simply another maladaptive defensive pattern.

Sadness is not the only feeling we need to experience and express. Anger is also part of grieving. We are naturally angry and disappointed because we have suffered loss. It is cold anger that shuts us down and cuts us off from one another. We are often afraid of expressing anger. We do not want to hurt others or we fear that they will retaliate and that this might hurt us. Yet if we cannot openly acknowledge our anger, how are our loving expressions to be trusted. If someone can only express the nice side of themselves, how are others to know if their niceness is to be trusted. It is true that anger can be used as a defence. It may appear safer to express anger than to acknowledge hurt or vulnerability, and we can get stuck on blaming others or expressing our hurt and disappointment in anger, and avoid 'giving in' to tears and sadness. But our anger is important and its acknowledgement is an essential part of the healing process.

Similarly, we can get stuck on sadness and be unwilling to take the risk of acknowledging or expressing the anger which is also present, the energy of which might empower us to take necessary action.

This is particularly problematic when we allow ourselves to be constantly put upon. Out of generosity – or possibly from some fear of being seen in a bad light – it may be our habit to take on a lot that needs to be done or to be the one in every relationship who seems to give the most and is then let down. The time comes when we reach the limit of our endurance. Others betray us because they are not equally generous to us. They seem to have taken us for granted and we are victims of their ingratitude. When this is a recurring pattern, it is necessary to look at how well we take care of ourselves. It may be relatively easy to take care of others, but the implicit contract may well be that they in return should take care of us, something that may not always happen. The way out of such recurring disappointment and grief is to learn – and this is often learned painfully and with effort – to stop when one has given as much as feels good for oneself. It is better to say: 'I wouldn't feel good about doing that' rather than let yourself be taken for granted and end up angry and hurt because the other has taken so much. This can feel mean and ungenerous but the alternative is to end up blaming the other for meanness.

Sometimes, the other in this situation is relieved by our stand instead of angry, glad to see that we are better able to take care of ourselves than they thought. It relieves them of the burden of guilt and may even make it easier for them to come closer and offer more because they feel less threatened. They may have felt that more was needed from them than they could deliver because we took care of others and seemed to have overwhelming needs ourselves which we weren't taking care of but seemed to expect them to meet.

Anger has great energy. When we continually suppress our anger, we depress our energy. Suppressed anger can be associated with depression. Weighed down by things we feel we cannot stand up to, we sit on our anger but then feel disempowered and helpless. We may then feel that an explosion would be required to reverse the situation. Sometimes an explosion, or several explosions, are needed. If we express our anger at the time we first feel angry and need to address a difficulty, then such explosions are seldom needed. As with the tears talked about earlier, anger – like most feelings – is not so threatening when acknowledged and allowed to flow as the occasion arises.

We have a backlog of feelings relating to times we were hurt, disappointed, humiliated, put down and sad. We may have a backlog of feelings related to breavements and losses of every kind – from lost opportunities to the death of someone we loved dearly. It is this backlog of feeling that makes it difficult to allow ourselves the feelings of the present moment. As soon as we allow ourselves to feel anything at any depth, the baggage of the past joins in and intensifies the feelings of the moment. Anger or sadness in relation to a present difficulty is therefore much more intense than it would be were it not touching into similar feelings relating to past events.

Clearing the backlog is a task that is often undertaken in psychotherapy. Grieving the past and completing unfinished situations frees us to be more fully present in the here and now. Ultimately it may also free us to be a more open channel for the kind of love that seems to come from something greater than ourselves, and which is both within and beyond us.

Simply by addressing unfinished situations from the past we can encourage a lot of healing. To begin with, we may discover aspects of our means of dealing with hurts that may surprise us greatly. For instance, by addressing in imagination someone who has been important in the past, we may discover that although they left us long ago, we have not been willing to relinquish them. This may be at a stage when we no longer really need to hold on to them. Just coming to this realisation can sometimes be enough to enable us say 'goodbye' and let them go and with them a lot of our continuing pain.

From Gestalt therapy we have derived some very important ways of concluding our business with the past. The important point is to talk directly to the person or people involved: personally, as one to one, and very directly. This can be done by imagining them on a seat, or a cushion (which is often better) in front of you. Tell them all you need to say, particularly how much you miss them or how angry you are with them for leaving you or how hurt you feel by their actions. Remember that it is essential to talk in a direct and frank way and take lots of time to allow yourself experience and express the feelings that emerge in you. You could also do this by writing if it would be too daunting to do something as unusual or 'crazy' as talking to cushions.

When you have said all that you can think of, place a chair or cushion where you were and sit on the chair or cushion on which you had placed this person in your imagination. Just sit there quietly for a moment and gradually allow yourself to imagine that you are actually in their shoes and in their skin. Allow yourself to imagine how it is to sit here and listen to what has been said. Let the experience touch you. Respond – out of your imagination – with whatever arises in you as a possible response. Not out of what you think would be their response or what you imagine it should be. Just share what is present to you sitting in their seat. Share that directly with the chair or cushion opposite which is representing yourself. Share completely all that occurs to you including the associated feelings – this is important. Continue this dialogue, moving between these two positions until you feel that the process is complete and that there is nothing left to say either for now or for ever. It is a regular part of this experience to feel confusion. If you do so, then sit with the confusion. Do not try to work things out – just sit and then express whatever comes to you out of the confusion from either position and continue in this way.

This is a powerful healing process. It is not any kind of party exercise and should only be undertaken on your own or with someone you really trust. Do not try to analyse the experience, expecially at the time. Even more important, do not analyse such an experience for anyone else or allow them to do so for you. The experience will reveal its truth to you itself if you see it through. If you do try this, be prepared for feeling some strong feelings.

You may not have such feelings, of course, but it is best to know that you could. Be gentle with yourself.

Many kinds of past events or dreams can be explored in this way. It can be particularly effective in group therapy. However, such a process should be facilitated for others only by those who have a good deal of experience and know how to be present and see it through with others whatever may emerge. It is not just a simple technique. The important thing is to stay with what is happening. It is not appropriate to push. In particular, it is inappropriate prematurely to conclude 'unfinished' business – obviously it then remains unfinished.

There are people and things we all need to say goodbye to. We will do so at the right time. When all that has to be said is said and all that has to be learned is learned and when we are ready and have sufficient courage, we will be able to say goodbye to the past and be that much more ready to continue more fully in the present and to move forward to the future.

6

GOOD COMMUNICATION IS
THE LANGUAGE OF LOVE

Communication often takes place in a ritualised manner.

'How are you?'

'Fine thanks, how are you?'

Very few people actually expect to hear much about your wellbeing when they ask the question. Day to day, meeting people here and there, we exchange pleasantries and pass on. This can be a very frustrating experience if you are desirous of making a meaningful connection with another human being or when you are lonely and upset about something or full of the joy of a new discovery.

At the same time, it serves a useful purpose. We do not want to have to listen to everyone's story when we meet them, nor do we wish to pour our hearts out to everyone with whom we are acquainted. These initial pleasantries allow us acknowledge one another and make a little contact while also allowing us to maintain boundaries. So we reach out and at the same time, keep our distance.

Perhaps the next step forward in meeting another is enquiring specifically how something went or how someone got on at the hospital or wherever. Or, telling a bit about ourselves and recent happenings. We will then notice consciously or without realising it, when the other's attention begins to wander or our listening becomes less intent as our attention moves on to something else and the conversation gradually winds down.

There are different levels of communication. Depending on the level, we make greater or less contact with the other. Usually, the more general the content of the conversation, the more distance we will preserve and the more intact we will keep our personal boundaries. The more direct and personal we are, the more contact we will make and the more we will let down our boundaries and create the potential to move closer to the other. Usually we take our time and gradually discover if it is possible to move closer. We check out one anothers' attitudes and likes and dislikes and make some judgements about the likelihood of our being able to get on together.

Many people get on very well while hardly ever, or maybe never, directly telling each other how they feel about each other. They assume that their behaviour towards each other tells its own story and the fact that they share an unspoken understanding creates a further bond between them. Their ritualised way of communicating is understood by both of them and they see anything else as unnecessary and maybe even intrusive and a breach of their privacy. In a way, every family has its own ritualised way of communicating. In most cases the way our own family operates is what prescribes normality for us. Some families are very expressive and noisy; others are quiet and contained. Some make a lot of physical contact, while for others, physical contact would be rare and uncomfortable.

The way we communicate does not say anything about how much we love but it may effect the way another perceives our love. When people from different families come together, they may have difficulty in interpreting each other's signals. We are often drawn to those who are different from ourselves in these areas but this can increase the difficulty. Reticence in one person may give the impression of secrecy or an unwillingness to share, while another's questioning and persistent talking may seem invasive and disrespectful to the first person.

Some families share so much and are so apparently close that it can be difficult for members to develop their own boundaries – to have even a minimum amount of privacy and to develop a sense of themselves as distinct from the family. At the other end of this continuum, there are families who are so distant from each other that it can be hard for individual members to have much sense of belonging or contact. With every pattern of interaction there are advantages and disadvantages. Where we are strong in one way, it can be valuable to widen our territory by experimenting with being a little different. If you are very contained, it could be good to try to volunteer a little more in communication with others: if you are a great talker, you might try containing yourself a little more and sharing less. Any such changes are strange and uncomfortable at first, yet often give us the opportunity to discover something new about ourselves or about the way things can be.

Within families too, not everyone is comfortable with

the established pattern. The pattern itself is like a dance where people have accommodated each other and find their place and now keep repeating the same sequence of steps because they know it works. When one dancer steps out of line, everyone has to find a new accommodation so that harmony can be restored. At first they may try to pull that dancer back into line: 'That's not the way we do things here.' 'Don't talk like that.' 'Why are you so quiet.' 'You haven't been like yourself all week.' 'What's the matter with you?' 'Are you feeling all right?'

This makes it especially difficult to try something new, yet if one holds the new position long enough the other dancers will have to alter their step and find out how to dance with that response if they are all to come to some new accommodation and comfort be restored. It doesn't always have to be restored by resorting to the old familiar pattern. A new sequence can be established which can become equally comfortable in time. What is difficult is when the first dancer steps out but doesn't hold the new position long enough for others to accommodate her/him. By moving back and forth between the new and the old steps, perhaps because of uncertainty or fear or because of trying to accommodate everyone else, the dancer – the person wanting something new and different – does not give the system, the family members, time to find a new accommodation, which could turn out to be ultimately more satisfying for all concerned.

The ways in which we communicate are fundamental to the nature of the relationships we are part of. The contact we make with one another is through words, body language and touch. The degree of contact we make is directly related to the way in which we communicate. We convey our need to defend ourselves from others or our willingness to extend ourselves to others by the way we communicate, mostly through words. As has been said, much of our contact takes place through the ritualised communication that is part of our everyday lives. A lot depends on the interpretations we put on what is said. Those interpretations depend on our previous experience of life, of ourselves and of the other person.

Most of the misunderstandings that occur in life come from misinterpreting communication. Encounter groups and communication groups demonstrate repeatedly that when people stay together and talk things through in a group process even those who would normally have nothing to do with one another can become reconciled. This was particularly movingly demonstrated for Irish people by Carl Rogers in the film of the work he did with people from all sides of the Northern Ireland conflict. It has been reported that some scenes of reconciliation had to be removed at the editing stage because people felt they would be in danger at home if they were seen to have become so close to 'the enemy'. Communication is a crucial part of how we can come practically and genuinely to love our enemies.

Much has been learned from encounter groups and other group work about effective communication. Perhaps one should instead say affective communication. Because such contact involves the inclusion of emotions and a true expression of self. In such groups, people gradually come to share many underlying fears and assumptions. One of our biggest fears is that we would not be accepted if known for who we really are. In such groups people often discover that their worst judgements of themselves are not shared by others. The question regularly arises 'Can the people in this group accept me?' Then, 'Can I trust the group?' 'Are the people in this group to be trusted to tell the truth or are they just being nice?'. Or: 'If someone here does not approve of me, does that mean they're right or could I be right too, at least for me?' and 'Whose opinion matters most in the end anyway; whose opinion do I actually act upon in my life?'

By taking the risk of being honest, people reveal more of themselves. When they encounter similar honesty from others they have a real sense of meeting and making contact that may seldom, if ever, be part of their lives at other times. Where the group can work through a lot of conflict and deal with their reservations and judgements as well as their appreciations, the experience can become a loving one, where people can feel accepted and cared for by others just as they are. Here people dare to reach out and touch one another both by understanding words and direct statements of appreciation and love and by offering hugs or a hand to hold or a shoulder of support to cry upon.

It is astounding that any group that initially comes together and talks in the ritual style will always turn out to be full of people living lives of courage and fear, heartbreak and inspiration. They often feel alone or different or strange until they discover, within the safe confines of a confidential setting, that we are all vulnerable, all fearful and for the most part, doing the best we can with what we have.

We live in a strange world where we implicitly collude with the myth that to acknowledge vulnerability is to acknowledge weakness. Weakness implies failure. Yet the truth is, whether we acknowledge it or defend ourselves by denying it, that we are all vulnerable and all need to feel accepted, appreciated and loved. True strength comes from having the courage to acknowledge vulnerability. Denying vulnerability we deny ourselves – not daring to be present to others or ourselves as we really are. Discovering ourselves vulnerable yet willing to be openly present, we discover the strength of vulnerability and the door to contact, intimacy and love.

We know that there are some aspects of communication that create the optimum conditions for contact, conflict-resolution and intimacy. The first is the importance of listening. Often, while listening to another, we are planning our reply or thinking of other things which are evoked in us by what we are hearing. To take a first step, make sure you hear what the other person is actually saying. You may assume that they mean one thing but be aware that there are other possibilities. Ask. Check out. It is often a very good idea – especially in a situation of misunderstanding or conflict – to say back to the person what you understood them to say and check out with them if this is what they meant. Listen to their response and to differences in the nuances of meaning that may be present.

Having clarified that you have heard what they intended to say, then it is time to give your response. It is always helpful to acknowledge other people's feelings and we are not encouraged or trained to do so. Where someone presents their feelings of fear or anger, we often try to reassure them by telling them there's no need to be afraid or angry, or by giving them reasons why they need not, or even should not, be angry, sad or whatever. This is not always experienced as reassuring and can often be seen as dismissive. Sometimes the only person it reassures is the speaker.

Instead it is helpful and respectful simply to acknowledge hearing the person describing their feelings. 'I can see you feel scared', or 'I recognise you're angry' or 'That's obviously very upsetting to you'. Make no judgement but do acknowledge the feelings. When you have grasped what the fear, anger or sadness is about, it is then appropriate to give your own response. This should clearly indicate your own beliefs and feelings about the situation while still clearly acknowledging the other's beliefs and feelings. It can be very tempting, whether consciously or unwittingly, to imply that your own reaction would be the correct one or a better alternative to what has been presented. We often assume that only one solution, or one way of looking, or one attitude is appropriate. So an alternative can sound like a put-down. It is helpful therefore to take clear responsibility for our response. 'If it were me, I think I'd feel . . .' 'I don't think I'd see it that way', or 'I think I would feel the same way if I were in your shoes.' Loving communication is helped by an attitude which says: whether I agree or disagree, I uphold your right to your own opinion – your opinion, your feelings are important because you are important.

The following are simple guidelines for clear communication that help to foster good relationships and facilitate conflict-resolution.

The first guidline is to speak for yourself using 'I' statements. Instead of politely talking in general terms, using 'I' makes it clear that you are speaking for yourself and not assuming that what you are saying is also true for the other. Because general statements are more socially correct, our personal communication often comes unstuck because it is laced with assumptions. You can end up having a serious row about something silly like how someone cooks something just because you don't differentiate between your own likes in this regard and the other person's.

A second guideline concerns the use of questions. Very many questions arise in the mind because of a thought that has occurred. So many questions hide behind an implied statement: 'Have you ever thought of taking French classes?' instead of 'I think French classes would be a good idea' or 'I've often though I'd like to learn French'. We know implicitly that many questions are asked to elicit a particular expected answer so we play defensive games by trying to answer the assumption we presume is behind the question. Life gets very complicated in the ensuing confusion. If the subject matter is sensitive for the people involved, a row can erupt in this way, leaving the protagonists wondering how on earth it all started.

We spend a lot of time mind guessing each other, responding to what we believe is behind one another's words without really knowing. Simply telling the other what you think they're thinking brings some surprises. 'You said you're tired. I assume you mean you want me to do the washing up, do you?' could lead to 'No, I'm tired and I'd love to sit here with you quietly for a while before getting up. Then I'd actually find the washing up a relief after all the talking.' Obviously much more serious assumptions could regularly benefit from being checked out in this way too.

Simply speaking for yourself, sharing feelings honestly without blame or justification, checking out assumptions and then checking them out again and again can make a very big difference in many situations. When we simply speak our truth to each other honestly and drop our defences we may not have the same perceptions or be able to agree, but great reconciliation can still take place. When we feel heard and recognised and respected and when we can offer the same respect to another, much of the pain of conflict is eased. When I talk directly to you using 'I' and 'You', we make contact. This will not always be painless but if it is real and genuine, then, at very least, we support each other in our pain. In this genuine communication both are vulnerable. When we are able to trust each other with our pain and difficulties, pleasures and joys in this way, we will be blessed with moments of grace where true healing is possible in a climate of love and understanding.

7

RELATIONSHIP – THE LOVE CRUCIBLE

Love is always about relationship. In this sense, relationship, as we said earlier, is the antithesis of alienation. We
cannot talk about love except in relationship. Our journey
to love is a journey to connect and reconnect with the web
of relationships of which we are part. It is a journey to
connect at many different levels and when we have made
the connection at one level, then we are called on to
discover and reach further depths. By following this
process, we are led from one connection to another to the
loving core and, thus to the love that is source of our
being, both within us and beyond us in the world, or
maybe even worlds, outside.

Each of us is really a system of interrelated parts. This
is true of our bodies, it is true of our psyche and, of
course, it is true of the whole. This living system is part
of a web of relationships on all kinds of levels. We are a
part of the natural world and despite all our attempts to
control it, we are deeply affected by our relationship, or
lack of relationship, with it. We are part of networks of
relationships with people: families; friends; schools;
societies; work networks; interest networks; cultures and
so on. Even when we are not practically relating to these

networks, if we are isolated in some way, we still carry our knowledge of them with us and so are still in relationship. The way we communicate affects the level of connection we make. So does the level of commitment we make and the length of time we stay in relationship.

If 'love is an alchemical process in which we are the material to be transmuted' then relationship is the vessel holding the process. All relationships have potential in this way but marriage can be particularly effective in challenging our ability to relate and to love. The love that brings two people to commit themselves to each other goes on to challenge them to grow and develop in myriad ways. It is an alchemical process in that it has the potential to turn base metal into pure gold.

This kind of transforming relationship is not static. It must involve the partners in many struggles. It has been suggested that the deeper the sense of connection between the couple, the more they experience themselves as soul mates, the more the relationship will be likely to challenge them. If so, it is perhaps because they know they can love each other in a deep way and are challenged then to clear all that gets in the way of their ability to express that love.

It may be that when we make contact with love through relationship or meditation or prayer or some other peak experience, we know in a very real way what is possible and constantly have to face the challenge of clearing out the attitudes and feelings and ways of being that block us from loving. Thus the experience of deep love itself becomes the catalyst – the motivation – for us to work toward materialising love in our lives. Such an experience awakens us to the deep longing within us for love and for the spiritual sustenance that we may avoid in so many other ways – by activity, addictions, greed and so on.

What we may come to realise in time is that much of the love we feel early on in relationships may be based more on our need for love than on our ability to love. Our sense of loving someone is experienced as a yearning for them. Feeling loved by them is also such a wonderful experience that we love them for loving us. There may never be occasion to question the basis of our loving. But when we are challenged by difficulties to take a look at what is happening, we may discover that our need for love and the way we express our love are influenced by many factors. For example, many people who suffer abuse or ill-treatment in relationships often ask themselves why they continue to put up with the abusive aspects of the relationship. Partly it is because they know it could be different. They know this behaviour is only one aspect of their loved one's personhood and they love the person behind the abuser. However, they also often have to look at how their need to love (to take care of) and their need to be loved by the other is holding them almost like an addiction in a relationship that may be damaging them – sometimes so severely that their lives and the lives of their children may be at risk.

This is an extreme example but we are all dependent on one another to some degree and this dependency can manipulate relationships. The message is: I will love you in certain ways on condition that you will love me in others. Such a contract is usually implicit and out of our awareness.

Some years ago there was much debate about a change

in the Irish constitution that would allow for divorce legislation. There was a great deal of emphasis put by those opposed to the introduction of divorce on how insecure women would be if their husbands could leave them. Listening to the debate, one could at times form the impression that many marriages were held together only by legal contract. It raised the question as to whether these women (or husbands for that matter, but this was not so much implied at the time) would really want to keep partners who no longer wished to be with them. For what reason would they wish to do so? Presumably because of the ways they depended on the relationship – financially perhaps, but also emotionally. This raises questions about the level of self-esteem involved. Were there really so many people whose spouses would leave them immediately they got the chance to be free from the contractual straitjacket or was this fear based on insecurity that came from feeling 'Nobody could really love me, just for myself – especially once I get past being young and stereotypically attractive.'

What kind of love and respect do we feel for ourselves when we are desperate to keep people in relationship with us? Of course insecurity and feelings of inadequacy are created and fed by an abusive partner, so it is no wonder that people do come to feel this way. It highlights how much we fear loneliness, depend on others for self-esteem and don't trust ourselves enough to know that we could be OK alone and also be able to offer something to new people and form new relationships.

Dependency is part of loving. We need to be loved and to love. When we do love we are vulnerable to the pain of losing the loved one or to being hurt by the way they act.

We can, however, also be secure in ourselves to a greater or lesser extent and this affects the way we love and experience love. Long-term relationships can challenge us in our loving. They can challenge us to make unconditional love a more regular part of our loving and to look at the conditional loving we offer and the conditions with which we collude in order to feel loved.

There are moments when we do love unconditionally: special moments when we hold our child and feel our heart swell with love or make contact with another in a moment of intimacy. Then we experience ourselves as fully loving in the moment with no expectations – either of the other or of ourselves. These are moments when we just open ourselves and love is present. However, most of the time in our relationships, particularly where there is the possibility of a romantic engagagement, we are planning or wondering about the future or the implications of the present instead of just enjoying the relationship as it is right now.

When we first meet someone and go for a walk or go out for a meal together, we can be wondering whether we'll meet again, whether we'd want to meet the other person again, whether we might make some commitment to each other, whether we'd be willing or they'd be willing to make love, how far that might go, what the implications might be . . .

While these speculations are part of the excitement of attraction they can also become means for us to frighten ourselves. We shun the risk of being present for fear of the assumptions that will be made in the future. Before even getting to know each other, we may decide not to meet again for fear the other will want to get more involved than we do or for fear we will get too involved and be rejected or for a host of other reasons that relate to the future. We complicate relationships hugely with all this speculation, and make it really difficult to enjoy contact and communication with others for its own sake.

Much of what happens between individuals is implicit and never verbalised. It makes things immeasurably easier if we can discuss the worries and fears. Sometimes, however, such discussions are motivated by the need for security. We want to know if we get involved (that is, if we begin to feel love for, or loved by, the other) that the other will be there for us. We don't want to risk investing ourselves in a relationship for fear of the pain of rejection and loss. This fear can lead us to seek more than can realistically be committed too early or to avoid spending too much time with someone for fear they will expect commitment from us. It can then short-circuit the relationship process and bring about the very rejection we fear. Much potential nourishing contact is lost in this way. When we discuss our fears, we need to acknowledge the fear of being rejected but not by seeking premature commitment from the other that they will stay. It is more useful to ask for a commitment to a good leavetaking, should it become necessary, than to pretend it couldn't happen.

Relating is always a risk. In some ways, the more we are able to risk and able to let go, the more we are open to receive love and the more likely we are to find it. One useful approach is to make short-term contracts, which can be regularly renegotiated, to agree the parameters of the present relationship, for instance, agree that we enjoy spending time together and that this does not imply commitment to romance even though it does not necessarily exclude such a possibility.

The more explicit you can be with the other person, the more safety will be built in to allow you to enjoy the relationship in the present. Honesty is often the best kind of security to offer and give. Avoid the temptation to ask or give commitments about how you will feel in the future. It would be great if we could know, but feelings are feelings and they can vary quite a lot in the process of a relationship.

Contracts around sexual contact can be especially helpful even though difficult to discuss. The process of participating in these kind of contract discussions also builds relationship and intimacy in that it involves risk-taking, honesty, vulnerability and clear communication – all major factors in intimacy. Agreements can be reached to exclude sexual contact, or to include some sexual intimacy when appropriate (for example, when both partners feel like it, or only in certain circumstances), but to exclude a full sexual relationship. You might like to agree on nourishing physical contact such as hugs and holding, and avoid more sensual or erotic contact. Other options agreed on might be for sexual passion to be given full expression when it arises but that there will be no commitment involved or alternatively that a full sexual relationship is only to take place, if ever, when commitment is there. The nature of commitment needs also to be made explicit. Commitment can mean many different things to people. 'Commitment to what?' is a really important question. To honesty, to not having sex with anyone else while remaining in this relationship, to a long-term relationship, to marriage . . . ?

Be honest, be explicit, be realistic in your commitments. That is, commit only to what you can honestly deliver. If you or your partner can't commit to anything, then that's useful to know and while it makes the relationship very risky, at least it doesn't offer false promise.

In the short-term, fears about commitment need to be overcome to allow us engage fully with – in the sense of being fully present to – each other. Premature worries need to be seen for what they are and may need to be put on one side if we are to have time even to begin to get to know one another in a relaxed way. Longer-term issues of commitment become important in other ways. Some people have particular difficulty in making a commitment.

This fear of commitment seems to be a fear of engagement. The fear of becoming engaged in a long-term relationship may itself mean having to become engaged with oneself and another in a process of loving. This kind of engagement can confront us with our addiction to alienation. Relationship requires one to be present, not only to oneself but to another. To make it work, we have to look at the ways we relate. Some of us fear the imagined loss of freedom. This seems to mean the freedom to be free, to come and go as we please, to do what we like, when we like, without consequences for another. This freedom also has its limitations. It denies us the possibility of really knowing and being known by another. It denies us the possiblity of being held by a loving relationship which can also transform us. The boundaries that contain a long-term relationship, such as marriage, could actually confront us more with the limits within ourselves and the way those define us than constrain us from doing things we want or need to do. Sometimes the need to roam free stems from our limited ability to accept ourselves and to love, and this is more constraining than any relationship would be. Within a relationship these self-imposed limits might be challenged. Sometimes commitment in relationship leads to freedom.

Such fears, however, do raise questions about what we believe a committed relationship entails. Often stereotypical notions of marriage need to be challenged – most of all in ourselves. Marriage as an institution has changed considerably. This brings new possibilities but also new challenges. In the past, getting married involved taking on a clearly defined role. In some ways, marriage had more supports in that less was expected from it. Within closely knit communities, other supportive relationships were available too. Nowadays we often put huge stress on marriage by expecting the relationship to answer so many of our needs. It is unrealistic to expect all our needs to be met by our partner. Marriage does not have the same community supports it used to have, so we also need to nurture ourselves by investing in other relationships – offering different things – thereby nourishing our ability to give more to others and to our primary relationships.

The great advantage of the present time is that we can no longer easily assume we know the form marriage will take. It is more obviously necessary to talk about the kind of contracts we are making. Never has it been so important to make the implicit assumptions explicit. In the last decades women fought to have their husbands accept their need and right to have the option to work outside the home as well as in it. Nowadays their husbands may just as easily assume that they will take equal responsibility for the family finances and the assumptions of both partners about who will do what household chores or take what parental roles may be very different. A relationship can no longer be safely based on such assumptions about husband and wife roles.

Once again, discussion of the contract is essential. In a loving relationship which supports growth and development, such discussion and contracting needs to form an integral part. In a committed relationship, the early months and maybe years will involve finding a comfortable accommodation with one another and establishing the pattern of the relationship. All being well, such a pattern may last a long time. Often we marry someone who has opposite strengths to our own which, at least at first, we value and appreciate. So very responsible people often marry characters who are easy-going or have a dare-devil quality about them or very shy people choose a partner who is the life and soul of the party. This is great until the quiet member begins to feel ignored because of her partner's gregarious behaviour, while the gregarious one may feel too much leaned on and tied to home. Early on in the partnership it's great to have a partner whose skills and inclinations complement one's own. Later on, however, we may find them difficult to understand or, even more likely, they may come in the way of the development of the undeveloped side of ourselves.

The quiet partner may decide to 'develop herself' and

go out and join a women's group, learn assertiveness or develop a new talent or get a job or any combination of these, and develop a life of her own. Stronger in herself, she may begin to want more independence. She may want to have more say in engagements or begin to make new relationships apart from her partner when they go out. He may begin to feel vulnerable, even jealous, and badly treated. He may withdraw into himself and become quieter and want to stay at home. They need to find a new way of relating to each other that allows for her new ventures and gives him space to be quiet some of the time. Or he may continue to feel unappreciated or put down and she may feel confined and stereotypically controlled as a woman. At stages like this, parts of ourselves that have been invested in the other, or in the relationship, may need to be recovered. Some of the ways the couple were interdependent may need to be dropped as each person recovers parts of themselves that were lost or hidden from view.

As this happens it can feel as if the relationship is falling apart and there is a danger that it will not be able to survive. In many ways, the relationship is not surviving because the old one does need to be let go in order for the couple to find a new and more satisfying way of being together. However, the challenge is to continue renegotiating the contract and for the individuals within the relationship to allow enough scope for their own and the other's development. Once again, as life keeps teaching, we need to be able to let go and in so doing, may actually get to discover that we can have even greater riches than before.

If we allow the old relationship to 'die', remain open to what happens next and continue to accompany our partners on their life's journey, a new relationship may often be established that is even better than the old. The individuals may discover more in themselves than they previously appreciated and be able to become fuller selves, and to be a partner to the other in a more autonomous and respectful way. In this process it is our commitment and love which enables the transformation to take place – both of the partner and the relationship.

Often what we admire, or even dislike, in our partner we may have to discover and/or develop in ourselves and this begins to shift the balance of the relationship, challenging the other partner to look at what they need to recover for themselves. There are some further issues that we can explore through the example given above.

Gender issues are a fundamental part of every relation-ship. How I see myself, and how you see me, as a woman, affects the way you relate to me. How I see the masculine side of myself is also important. Whatever gender we are, we have the opposite aspect within us as well. So, as a female, I have a masculine side to my nature as well as a feminine and the way these aspects are balanced is important in my development if I am to move toward greater whole-ness. Similarly, of course, my partner has a feminine aspect to his nature as well as the masculine.

When women move forward in their development, most often (although not necessarily) they need to develop their strength. Like everyone they need to develop an ego and a strong sense of the 'somebody' that is them. Moving into feelings to grieve losses and recover the inner child may come easier to women than to men because they are socially more supported in their ability to feel. The message given is that it is all right to have feelings if you are a woman – or at least, less all wrong. The struggle for a woman – and it is still some struggle – is to attain a place in the world that is right for her as she may well have to fight all sorts of norms which suggest that only certain places could be right for her because she is a woman. In doing that she develops her strength. The critical challenge is to manage also to retain and develop the core of herself. Because of macho conditioning, she will also come under great pressure to become more male than the men in order to prove herself. She will not be asked to prove herself as a woman person but as a person who will be assessed in male terms. Of course this has disastrous consequences for the world because the world needs women now to redress the balance of power and bring forward the feminine aspect. Macho women will change nothing. Woman power is about women coming from the place of power within themselves.

Very often, because their struggle is so great in the first place, women who are successful (in the world) have undertaken a lot of self-development in order to recover confidence in their ability to take on the odds that are so often pitted against them. In this process they may recover much of the depth of themselves that was lost or injured in their growing to adulthood and so they can be powerful in a centred way. They have often discovered in their struggles that power comes from power within, from being centred as close to the core of oneself as possible. Real power is about the ability to deal equally with people. It is not vested by institutions, it is not power over others – although one may hold positions of power – but comes from knowing oneself and being able to acknowledge the importance of oneself and the importance of the other and meeting from a place of respect of self and other.

Men, on the other hand, have often been socialised to believe that power comes from being 'somebody': from the position they hold in the world; from competing and winning and thus from being higher up the hierarchy. All their training may have implicitly been about the need to obtain position and hold onto it. It is often therefore hard for them to find their own real male power. The pseudo-macho power is so pervasive that it blinds them to the real possibilities within themselves.

For men to recover their male power – the 'wild man' within – they have first to surrender their investment in the 'somebody' (as we all do, but women may have not had so much position attached to their 'somebody'). They have to recover feelings, and are often faced first with the need to get 'permission' to have feelings and to reclaim the ability to feel. Then their grieving and the recovery of their core selves can begin. For men the immediate motivation for this process may not initially be so great because where women can now see how opportunities in society are closed to them, just because they are women, the issues may not be so obvious to men. The opportunities closed to men are less obvious because they are less valued in this macho society.

The inflated narcissistic self that is a defence against feelings of inadequacy was discussed in Chapter 3. All men's conditioning, within a society where such a defence has become the ideal, is to develop such a persona. Men are asked not to feel, told that men are not afraid, not weak, not vulnerable and so on. To be a successful man in society, the implication is that one has to collude with this falsehood and develop a self that denies the feelings of vulnerability, inadequacy and fear that are part of being human. The journey to recovery means standing out against the prevalent cultural myth and acknowledging the truth of oneself which, society will immediately suggest, makes you less of a man. Less of a man because 'manhood' is defined in a particularly false way. Of course this is also true for women in that women who refuse to hide their strength and power any longer are given all the messages that suggest they are less than female.

'For millennia men have been trying to overcome their fear of female power by controlling the lives of women,' says Frank Pittman in *Networker Journal*. Such an obvious statement, yet so seldom said. Most women recognise this fear immediately. We know men are afraid of our power. We know all the ways we are rejected and subtly, or not so subtly, 'put in our place' when we openly take power.

On some level the women's movement, far from challenging true male power, is challenging false male power and giving men respect by demanding that they overcome their fear and meet women equally. Women no longer need to collude in pretending that men are powerful while they hide behind macho images, pretending to be bigger and stronger than they feel. Women who have discovered their own power are no longer willing to offer men false security. They have taken the courage to explode the myth. They are tired of second place, of the abuse they suffer from fragile male egos, but they are also tired of the loneliness that comes from relating to a false image. Many such women feel deep grief about what has happened to men as well as women. They want to relate to real men.

In protecting men from their fear, women nearly lost themselves – they began to forget what they were about and believed the myth themselves. Their message to men is that it is time for men also to uncover their strength. Women do not want macho men, they do not want the weak-kneed wimps men are afraid they will become without their armour. Women want men to recover their vulnerability and the strength that comes from within. They want men who have the courage to stand in the strength of their vulnerability, who are willing to acknowledge the power of just being themselves: males – powerful and vulnerable, just as an erect penis stands potent, vulnerable and undefended, yet undeniably male.

Women have had the courage to step beyond the old relationship. The risk was, and is, that the relationship could not extend itself sufficiently and make room for whole people. Those committed to a new relationship – to trusting the process and to new possibilities – believe enough in themselves and know that men can take them as they are in their power. They want also to see men in their power. Such women might say to men: 'Walk tall in your own strength and meet us in a new way. We can then each have room for all of ourselves and live in a richer relationship of equality where love can thrive and where we can all continue to develop in love.'

Relationships of trust in which we are not afraid to

acknowledge both our vulnerabilities and strength foster intimacy, respect and independence. Both partners have the security of knowing they can stand on their own feet and yet can be involved in an intimate committed relationship. The relationship need not depend on avoiding fear by holding on to familiarity but can challenge the partners to face their fears, each with the support of the other.

8

Experiencing Love through the Body

Just as our DNA molecules hold the information which guides our growth and makes us develop into a human rather than some other kind of species, and a human with particular tendencies and abilities at that, so too we could have information within ourselves about the path in life which it is appropriate for us to follow for our lifetime. This path would unfold before us as life goes on. It has been suggested that life itself has contained within it an implicit order which is unfolding as the universe develops. (David Bohm, *Wholeness and the Implicate Order.*) Within ourselves we may well know what our journey is, or tasks are, for our lifetime, on some level we can't yet clearly name. This 'knowing' might include a destiny to be present to certain events or it might simply be that there are certain kinds of learning or transforming opportunities that will be part of our journey.

These learning opportunities or transforming experiences may concern the alchemical process of continuing to transform base metal into gold. If love, or a tendency to, or for, love, is the closest to a description of our core nature and if love is also a transforming experience through which we are transmuted, perhaps what is happening is an ongoing process of transformation and this process is actually what we are.

This image of base metal being turned into gold by an alchemical process suggests a purpose of refinement: a coarse substance being transmuted into a more refined and qualitatively purer substance. We know what it means to say that someone has a heart of gold. It tells us something about their ability to love. So on some level, it is being suggested, as our life happens, there is a tendency in us towards love and that tendency itself has also a tendency for transmutation into a purer and greater love, perhaps what we might call Spirit. Or, perhaps, this more refined energy is more compatible, more at home with the energy of the Spirit.

This way of speaking can be very far away from our everyday experience of living. However it suggests that somewhere within us there is a tendency for something to happen in our lives which needs to be faciliated if we are to be most in tune with our true nature. When we live in tune with our nature – when we are not going against what it is our nature to be – then we are most likely to be healthy and to have a greater sense of peace and a greater capacity for wholeness.

It may also be that this tendency for transforming ourselves in love will continue to pull at us, trying to get our attention whether or not we have any awareness of it. The more we go against it, the rougher the waters we will travel. It is easier to travel with the flow of the water than against the current.

The image of a homing device is helpful here. The draw of the homing device guides whatever is being called home to itself. How does the homing device within us work.? How do we know, minute to minute, where we are being directed and can we even hear any such message? If there is such a homing tendency within us how do we become aware of it and how can we use it to show us our way?

> You have eyes – can't you see?
> You have ears – can't you hear?
>
> Mark. 8:18

What might we be called to hear or to see that is not immediately obvious to our ordinary consciousness and how do we use our eyes, ears and bodies to become aware of that which is hidden?

Our alienation from the core of our selves leaves us confused in our search for direction. Yet the closer we come to recovering the self, the more events fall into place easily and lead us one from another, the more there is a sense of being guided, of being in contact with the energy of the call home – a call of love.

In our uncertainty about our place in the world, where do we begin? We begin with what we know. Honesty is the guiding principle, especially honesty with oneself. 'The truth shall set you free' is not a saying to be taken lightly. What do you know from your own experience to be the truth? Here one is asked to listen to experience, not just absorb the theories and thoughts of others. What we make of our experiences, how we interpret them to ourselves, is also influenced by previous events and explanations of reality. So it is valuable to separate your experiencing of yourself from the explanations you have given yourself of those experiences – to the extent that this is possible. An experience, in the way it is being spoken of here, is something perceived or felt by the body: an image seen by the eye, a sound heard by the ear, a feeling as a bodily sensation, an emotion or a sense of something which is intuitive or perceived through the imagination.

We spend a lot of our life trying to ignore our experience. We're hungry, and we tell ourselves it is the wrong time to eat; we're not hungry yet; it is mealtime and we eat, regardless of being already full. We mislead ourselves similarly with the need for rest, exercise, excitement and so on. When we listen sufficiently to our bodies they can tell us a lot about our real needs and yet we tune out their signals because we are willing only to let our heads decide how we are to act. Sometimes our bodies react strongly and we follow the impulse but disclaim responsibility for the action by saying we 'got carried away'. We thus discount decisions unless we make them with our heads, consciously, yet so strictly control our other impulses that they must eventually rebel and insist on 'being heard' or 'getting their needs met'. As a result, we distrust such demands even more strongly, expecting them to be uncontrollable and unruly, whereas were we to take account of the messages within us on a regular basis, there would be less need for over-action or reaction.

This is particularly true of our sexuality. Depending on the relationship we have with our bodies, sexual activity can be an expression of alienation and addiction or an expression of love, contact and deep relationship. It may well be that much permissive sexual activity is more an expression of alienation and addiction than an expression of love. It may also be that such activity is fuelled by the excessive controls and prohibitions placed by restrictive authoritarian morality. Such conditions enforce a strict regulation of what is a natural part of our being. We are sensuous physical beings. Our sexuality provides much of the vitality of our existence. It provides excitement, nourishment, contact, communication and pleasure. Were we not alienated both from our bodies and our true selves, sexuality might not need such a degree of control: our sexual rhythm would be more naturally part of the expression of who we are and therefore be less unruly, explosive and apparently in need of control.

Sexuality should be part of the daily expression of our lives. Walking, breathing, eating, communicating, dancing and loving are all sensuous experiences. Our contact with the world around us is essentially sensuous. Much of the time we experience much less than we could because we close down our senses for fear of being excessively sensuous. In doing this, we diminish our capacity to experience the abundance of life and our connection with nature. Contact with the world and other humans comes through the body. The words and tunes we hear, the body movements we observe, the way people look, the physical contact we make through handshakes and embraces – all these things form an intrinsic part of our communication with others. We need contact; without it most of us could not survive very long and certainly not in a very healthy way.

When we withdraw from feeling and detach from our body selves, we increasingly isolate ourselves from contact with others. Without being aware of having done this, it can seem that the only way back is through sex. On some level, we may sense that contact is needed. Emotional contact is absent and so, as sex is often the only legitimate means of physical contact for adults (hugs and embraces are often relegated to childhood), adults with a desperate need for contact can become addicted to sexual activity, maybe even moving from one partner to another, desperately hoping to having their basic need for love and contact addressed but remaining for ever unsatisfied.

The initial withdrawal and detachment from the body comes from prohibitions that relate to feelings and from painful experiences which can still be felt when we are in contact with the body. To be in contact with another we have to be in contact with ourselves. The very contact we crave can become too painful to experience because it connects us with the pain within ourselves which has to be healed before we can bear the love we desperately want. This is the extreme situation but is also true to a greater or lesser extent for all of us.

This situation sheds light on our difficulty in accepting divine love fully. If we feel so inadequate ourselves, we feel that anyone – even God or the Goddess – who loves us, either must have something wrong with them (hence they are not divine) or must be lying or cheating us because we know we are not lovable. No amount of persuasion on the part of another will change this until in some way our own perception changes, although the persistence of another may encourage the change in our perception.

Secondly, if we are to let love in it will touch us. The pain of our history will be touched and what we encounter along with love will be pain and, probably, sadness. Depending on our histories, the pain can be severe. This is the pain we need to heal so that we can cope with love. Divine love is so warm and so powerful that we are terrified of it. Such love would put us in touch with all the pain that separates us from the core. In doing so it would put us in touch with our grief; it also has the capacity to heal us completely, a transformation of which we are also terrified. Familiarity has great security and much of the time we live out of the rule: 'the pain you know is better than the pain you don't (know)'.

The body has its own innate wisdom and we learn to tune out its messages. Our experiences of life affect our bodies and so, when we have been through painful or traumatic experiences, we often numb off parts of the body rather than experience the pain. In fact this is the way we keep going, particularly when the events seriously threaten our security. We could not continue if we let these feelings of pain and threat overwhelm us. The survival of children depends on the adults – their parents or substit-ute-parents – being there to care for them literally in order for them to survive. If these adults, on whom they depend, turn out to be a danger to them, rather than a secure form of support, the threat will be so great that memories of it are naturally cut off. We cut off like this to a greater or lesser extent all our lives – cutting out, numbing off, leaving to one side the painful experiences or the parts of our selves we do not want or have no room for in our lives.

This has an effect on our bodies as well as our minds. There is no real separation between the two. Figures of speech reveal something of what is being said here. Think of phrases such as: 'Keeping a stiff upper lip'; 'back-breaking'; 'just trying to keep one's head above water'; 'standing your ground'; or 'keeping the ground under my feet'; 'keeping your head up' . . . Our bodies are part of who we are and the structure of our bodies (as in posture and the way our musuclature holds us) is formed along with our personalities.

Two basic patterns predominate. Many of us have what might be called 'overbound' structures: we tend to have a solid body structure with a quality of density. At the opposite end of the scale there are those whose body structure would tend more towards collapse. Both of these structures can be thought about in terms of energy. In the first instance, the energy can be seen to be contained well and bound within the body, while in the second case, the more collapsed structure, there is less capacity for energy to be held and more of a sense of lack of nourishment. People with the overbound structure are more likely to tend towards a more solid defence pattern, while those of the other type would be more likely to tend towards a placatory style of defence.

The structures of the body and the way we physically present ourselves in the world are part of who we are, the ways we interact with the people around us and the way we defend ourselves.

We *are* very much our bodies. The more we know of our selves – our body selves – the more we have the potential to break through the rigidities of our personalities to greater depths within. In this process, we can discover the innate wisdom of the body and the more we learn to listen to the messages our bodies give us, the more it seems it can guide us.

We are not all the same. After basic needs for food, shelter and human contact are met, we have differing needs, or at least vary in the amount of certain things we need as distinct from other things. Similarly, we have different capacities and different abilities. A lot of the time we try to behave as we have learned to do, regardless of our own unique properties.

We can begin to listen to our bodies in very simple ways, for instance allowing ourselves to be aware of our need for rest, or for food, for nourishment or for quiet. Doing this can cause problems. For example, our bodies may have need for rest, but we may dread stopping, for various reasons. Over the years, our self-esteem may have become dependent on action. If we are not active, not busy doing something, then we may feel useless. We justify our existence by being useful, by being someone who gets things done or who does things for everyone around. Then when the body protests and it is time to draw back from so much activity, we feel worthless. Sometimes illness or accidents have the positive benefit of making it impossible for us to continue in the same way and confronting us with the urgent need to look at what we are doing. Of course this is toughest and hardest to bear for those who are most invested in action. Yet it may also be the only way those people can be brought to a standstill and forced to consider their position. The tragedy is that because we look at health and ill-health in such a narrow way, the potential of such serious events in our lives may be missed.

Physical health should not be separated from whole health. Physical ill health could be seen as possibly the last manifestation of poor health. In the past, Chinese medical practitioners were paid only when their patients remained healthy. We assume that we are healthy and take good health for granted. Yet more and more advances in medical knowledge show the influence of lifestyle and eating patterns on health. Low income, with all its attendant problems, is a major factor in health. Social conditions and emotional wellbeing are recognised as significant factors. So, it could be suggested, are spiritual factors.

Eastern approaches to health refer to something that is best described as the flow of energy through the body and see it as a crucial factor. In China, it is described as *Ch'i*, as I will name it here. Ch'i is seen as fundamental to wellbeing. Tai Ch'i and the martial arts were ways of developing and facilitating Ch'i and were seen as spiritual practices. Physical symptoms can offer us a wider message as well as simply enabling us to identify the illness. When we are physically ill we should listen to these wider messages as well as treating the illness. Is there anything here our body might be trying to bring to our attention?

More usefully perhaps, it is worthwhile for us to consider health in a wider way while we are still apparently healthy. How do we respect our bodies? Sometimes we respect machinery more. Is this a measure of the level of respect we are willing to give ourselves?

Through body work therapies such as bioenergetics or biodynamic massage, we can come to know our embodied selves better. Yoga and Tai Ch'i offer other paths to physical self-knowledge. Sometimes, these paths are reduced in the western world to purely physical exercise classes. They can still be useful in that they facilitate physical wellbeing, but potentially, such classes can also offer a better awareness of the whole self and a meditative path. Such paths need not be at odds with a Christian outlook – rather they complement Christian practice by facilitating a deeper awareness of self – as distinct from ego self – and of the capacity for the Spirit of Truth which Christ promised would be available to all who wanted to be his followers.

With the help of bodywork, we can learn to release chronic holding patterns and defences and open ourselves further to the instinctive knowledge of the body which seems to bring us closer to the core loving self within. We cut off the full feeling capacity of our bodies most effectively by holding our breath. Deepening our breathing and staying still long enough to allow ourselves feel what is present is the beginning of body knowing.

As we reconnect with our bodies by listening to their messages, by honouring the feelings we have – about food, rest and nourishment, or, at a deeper level, feelings of grief or love or anger or fear – we reconnect further with the ground of our being, both in a core way within ourselves but also on the level of contact with the world in which we live. When we really feel ourselves in our bodies, we can literally feel the ground under our feet and this has a psychological effect. We need the ground under our feet for security and in order to sense our connection with the earth on which we live and of which we are a part.

Much of our fear in every aspect of life stems from a lack of security. This lack of security leads us in turn to behave defensively and prevents us from relating in a warm, loving way. Reconnecting in a fuller way with our bodies may confront us with feeling the fear or other feelings we avoid, but when we feel the ground under our feet we can come to know that it is safe to feel – whether it be fear, love or grief, sexual feelings, vulnerability, or power. By feeling the ground under our feet we know we can choose whether or not to act on the feelings. We can just allow them and feel them fully but know that we are in charge and that being in charge of our lives doesn't have to mean avoiding feelings.

Much of the time we are afraid of feelings because we do not separate having them from having to act on them. Feeling angry doesn't mean we have to attack; neither does a feeling of sexual attraction mean we are compelled to go to bed with the person who attracts us. Both these kinds of feelings, felt and acknowledged to oneself, can in fact assist honest relating. Unacknowledged, they can cause us to rationalise and put people or situations out of our lives for unjustifiable reasons which cause us and them pain and distress. Acknowledged, such feelings can deepen the relationship we have with ourselves and, potentially, with others. 'I know in my guts', is the phrase used to acknowledge body knowing. Not all of such knowledge comes from as deep within us as that gut sense, but learning to pay attention to such a sense guides us to a deeper wisdom than what comes from head knowing alone.

Relationships that acknowledge true feelings, however awkward they may be from time to time, are relationships built on truth. Such truth is the gateway to the soul. When we fully experience ourselves at one with our bodies and feel our connection with the earth, we seem also to rediscover our connection with the universe.

9

IMAGERY – A LANGUAGE FOR THE SOUL

Alienation is part of our everyday lives. There is a lot to suggest that we become addicted to this state of alienation while also longing for the sense of connection which is the deepest need of our beings.

We are challenged to live in an alienated world while taking on the task of recovering our connection with love. It may be the task of our species to recover and materialise this loving connection. As each person recovers sufficient connection with the loving process within themselves and becomes conscious of the process of self-transmutation that is taking place, that consciousness may add to the transmutation of consciousness that is taking place in our world. To 'redeem' the world we need to redeem – as in recover – ourselves. The more each of us can bring that consciousness of love to life, the more love will be available to assist us all to realise more of it in our lives. This may be a transformation process that continues to occur over generations and it is beginning to be possible for us to get a glimpse of it at this particular moment in history.

This is not to suggest that, consciously, we transform ourselves. Our task is to facilitate – to go along with – the transformation that the alchemical process of love is trying to bring about. Systems of all kind go through a cycle of change. They come to a plateau, then the balance of the system becomes upset again and this is part of the beginning of its further transformation. After a period of flux and apparent chaos, the new shape emerges and a new equilibrium is arrived at. This is true for us too.

If we listen to this urge for transformational change that continues to call us, then we will have periods of equilibrium – where we may experience real peace and a greater sense of wholeness – and we will go through periods of turbulence and seeming chaos where we are not sure who we are nor how our attitudes can be changing so drastically.

This is a cyclical process of death and rebirth. Regularly we may be called to relinquish the self we thought we were and open ourselves to the new self trying to be born.

When we follow the counsellor of truth, our inner process of development, and allow it to unfold even though we cannot see where it will take us, we are constantly allowing the (ego) self to die and a new self to be born. Security then can only be had by learning to trust this process. This means relinquishing our attachments to certainties about the world. It means being open to new learning, to relinquishing attachment to beliefs which may turn out to be blinkered although they offered great security. It may mean relinquishing attachment to certain life styles, to people, even to health. Ultimately, it must mean for each of us relinquishing life itself and surrendering our bodies to death.

In this process one's security comes from knowing oneself – from knowing one's connection with the source of the process which becomes the ground of one's being. Perhaps this is our connection with soul and it is as likely to appear to us through poetry, music, beauty, awe or chaos as through order, belief systems or conscious acts of will. Our addiction to security and certainty and thereby to control, can be the greatest barrier to this process.

Imagination is the window of the soul. Through it we can access knowledge and wisdom that is not available to us through thinking and feeling alone. Our most obvious connection with the imaginary world is through dreaming. The images in our dreams may reflect everyday concerns but they also reveal our subconscious concerns as well as occasionally touching on matters relating to wider events.

There are many ways of working with dreams. First there is the task of actually managing to recall the dreams we have had. As is well known this is best facilitated by taking time to write down, or record by tape, our memories as soon as possible after we dream. We can work on dreams in much the same way as the process of concluding unfinished business remaining from bereavement. This is only one possible way but it has the advantage that it allows all parts of one's psyche to be used without reducing them by giving them too narrow a focus – which can happen with some interpretative approaches.

With this gestalt process you can take any part of dream-person, object, environment and dialogue with it. Speak to that part and then speak for that part, maybe asking what it has to say to you. In the same way, different people within the dream might dialogue with each other or with different objects, and so on. Of course this requires an active use of one's imagination. You do not 'know' on a conscious level what the 'right' message is, but as you allow your imagination free in the dialogue it can be amazing to discover what you can know in another way. This can be very apposite to your life and can be discovered to fit very well when considered thoughtfully.

While it is important to get your head out of the way and allow the voice of imagination to speak, it is also very important to bring about an integration of these two aspects of knowing. This often occurs naturally but where difficulties occur, it can be good to encourage your thinking self to dialogue with the imaginary knower. So, for example, you might orchestrate a dialogue between your head and heart or between the voice of your imagination and your voice of reason. While they may not always be able to agree with one another, they can probably at least work out an accommodation. This is important, so that all aspects of yourself can be acknowledged and work together.

It is a simple step from dreams to fantasy. Just as our dreams can speak to us, so can images of fantasy. It can be a useful aid to creative problem-solving to seek images from within ourselves which can represent a difficulty to us. Sometimes when we relate to the images, whether by dialogue or simply by observation, an awareness of new possibilities can come from looking at the situation from this different perspective.

We can use images to meet different aspects of ourselves by allowing them to present themselves to us in this form. We can also use imagery to give ourselves subliminal messages for positive outcomes, for example, visualising ourselves in the mind's eye going through an event that we might be nervous about. In this instance, you would picture yourself going through the event looking calm and confident, see yourself performing well and

obviously enjoying yourself and then p
the event pleased and happy. This is the k
increasingly used to improve performan
can also be used to assist self-healing by
representation of an agent of healing workin
parts, also represented as an image, and se   ,rt
healed and restored. The final image you would give yourself
in this situation would be one of you enjoying yourself
somewhere after you've been restored to health.

Imagination can be used to increase confidence, reduce
nervousness and encourage self-healing. It can also be
useful though to allow images, of ill-health for example,
to surface themselves to see what they have to offer you.
One person with a severely itching rash tried this and kept
getting an image of a little spider-like creature. Diagnosis
took a long time but when scabies was eventually discovered to be the cause, the picture of the mite in a nurse's
dictionary coincided with the image received earlier.

Images do not necessarily show the actual problem in
this way; in fact they are more likely to present something
to you in a symbolic way. Here again it is useful to
dialogue internally with the image to find its message.
Questions such as how? or what? are often more helpful
than why? questions. This is because the why? question
requires a more abstract form of answer – more appropriate
to your thinking function – than the others. These facilitate
more readily the medium of the imagination.

Many forms of self-development use imagery inten-
sively. Analytical psychology uses the 'active imagination'
and psychosynthesis also places great emphasis on the
use of imagery in its approach to psychotherapy.

e 'Personal Totem Pole Process' is a particularly
ovely system of self-development based on the use of animal
imagery. The title comes from the totem pole of the
American Indians whose wonderful respect for nature and
what it has to teach us about spirit was nearly lost to
civilisation because to our lack of humility and inability to
listen and be open to unfamiliar paths of wisdom. This
system was developed by Steve Gallegos, a psychologist who
had already a great deal of experience using visualisation.

In the introductory workshop, participants are invited
to meet an animal for each energy centre of the body.
These energy centres are based on the chakras – energy
centres recognised by Eastern medicine and religions, and
which are central to an understanding of acupuncture. It
is suggested that each centre is related to different aspects
of the person, the most obvious being the heart chakra
which is thought to be related to matters of the heart,
such as love, loving and need for love.

Animals present themselves in different ways. A young
animal may suggest an aspect of the person that is new
or young or growing. An animal caged or injured obviously
suggests some kind of pain or lack of freedom, whereas
a strong healthy animal suggests strength. Again it is
important not to impose an interpretation on what occurs.
Unexpected possibilities may emerge through dialogue
with the animals. When the seven animals have been met
individually and are known through inner dialogue and
experience, they are invited to come together in council
or for healing. Their ensuing interactions can work
towards an accommodation and balance of different
aspects of the self, and following the process of their

journeying together can be very healing and supportive.

This process works on many levels. The animals can guide one on the level of ego by giving support and advice for dealing with life issues; they also facilitate intra-psychic activity and healing, sometimes by bringing one's attention to images from one's past and guiding one to do that which is necessary for healing. They also work on a transpersonal level, that is the level that goes beyond the person. So they can become a voice of inner knowing, speaking to us from the collective unconscious or the more obviously spiritual realms of the universe. They may present us with guides or other images of wisdom whose guidance may play a critical part in our continuing development and connection with what is divine, the love that is central to our lives.

As discussed in Chapter 4, this is the level at which, 'through deep imagery and intuition, we know ourselves in touch with something beyond ourselves and greater than ourselves which is also part of ourselves.'

The animals can become for us a connection with the Divine. In this realm of the psyche we open ourselves through deep imagery and intuition to the voice of divine guidance.

In *A New Vision of Reality* Father Bede Griffiths writes:

> . . . in the ancient world, as among the American Indians today, animals were conceived as part of the cosmic whole, in which trees and animals and human beings were all subject to the cosmic powers, the gods and angels, and to the supereme Spirit who pervaded all things . . . what we would consider to be subjective phenomena, experiences of the inner self, were then

experienced as objective realities. Gods and angels and all kinds of spirits and the Lord God himself, were all conceived as objective beings. Paradoxically, what we take to be objective, the phenomenal world 'outside' us, they conceived as a spiritual phenomenon, a psychic event and what we take to be subjective, our thoughts and feelings, they conceived as objective realities. This, of course, is simply due to the difference in functioning of the human mind, the reality itself is always beyond the sphere of the dualities.

In our modern world we have given little credence to the inner subjective world, but here we can see this was not always so. Today we need to learn to honour the subjective phenomenal world whilst also honouring the knowledge of our objective world. We need also to remember that reality encompasses both and attempt to transcend the boundary between objective and subjective truth.

There is difficulty here because, although we need to be able to acknowledge on some level that ultimately the phenomenal and objective world are part of a unity which encompasses both, it is essential for us to be able to hold the boundary. We cannot live in the objective world as if it were a subjective experience alone. A bus is a bus and if you walk in front of a moving one while experiencing it as a conglomeration of molecules you are still likely to be killed.

Through an engagement with the world which deep internal imagery can present to us, we connect more fully with the intermediary world between the natural world and that of the spirit. Here we may meet guardian angels, guides and archetypal images from many spheres. In this realm we may encounter wisdom but also demons and images of the shadow. It is important that we approach all these figures with respect but also in a matter-of-fact way. We need not reify or idealise these images and we need to be able to encounter them in the same way we encounter people in the human realm: opening ourselves to their wisdom and checking out thoroughly that which raises doubts in our minds. Visions and psychic experiences have something to say to us but they need to be incorporated into our everyday (personal) world of experience. Because we are not familiar with this realm, we sometimes make it too mysterious and dramatic. Precisely because we cut ourselves off from the possible ordinariness of everyday guidance from the deep intuitive level of knowing, we can give it too great proportion in our lives when we do connect.

Spiritual teachers warn against over-emphasising such experiences, often giving them little attention. When their followers mention them, they say, 'Not to worry, they will soon pass'. If our ego is too attached to such experiences, if they become self-inflatory, they are of little value to us.

However, most of us will meet these images without such drama. Where we do have experiences with a numinous quality they may well bring us healing and further transformation if we absorb the message they offer us. These may be experiences of deep prayer and meditation or may occur when we are absorbed in an intense experience of nature. However we encounter the divine in our lives, we are filled with a sense of awe and often gratitude for the love and wonder that accompany the experience.

10

COMING HOME TO LOVE
THROUGH MEDITATION

Many people have expressed their reaction to meditation as an experience of returning home. Meditation is thus a particularly apt way of reconnecting with the soul and the love that is central to life. It takes many different forms ranging from contemplative prayer to Yogic paths or Zen Buddhist practices.

Essentially the process is one of coming to a place where the internal chatter of the mind is stopped and we allow ourselves to enter into the stillness or the void. It is in fact a process of opening our hearts and minds to be able to 'hear' guidance and to access the guiding principle. Many books have been written about meditation and there are many different schools and teachers. So in this context various ways of beginning will be suggested.

Meditation normally takes place at times set aside when we sit still and focus attention. We may also have had moments of meditation which occurred of themselves and which we may never have named as such. For many of us these meditative moments come from experiences when we are close to nature: moments of awe or moments when the beauty of an evening or a landscape touches us deeply and we are quiet and know a stillness at the core of our being.

Such moments can also occur when at a time of intimacy, we feel really met by another: when the other, or others, seems to understand almost intuitively the depths of who we are and are able to be present, there in the moment with us. Such a moment was once described by a friend as 'bathing', because sitting in the stillness with such an intimate connection and just allowing oneself to feel all that is present, can be like what one imagines it would be to bathe the soul in a bath of love.

Such moments of beauty, peace and love feed the soul and we experience them as balm on our wounded and troubled hearts. Real healing can take place in such moments and they offer us a glimpse of what heaven could be.

This kind of intimacy can be experienced too as moments of true community, when the hearts and minds of a group of people are touched, perhaps by something someone has said, and a sense of openness and together-ness and at-oneness occurs. Such moments of grace are rare and would, ideally, be met by an appropriate ritual through which the group could celebrate together. When this is so, we can celebrate communion as a moment of shared love. Many of our present-day religious rituals may have come from such naturally occurring moments of communion.

Intimacy, whether in community or between individuals, comes from people being open to one another. Through honesty and the risk-taking that honesty demands, hearts are opened. This is the honesty that doesn't shy away from saying what it is difficult to acknowledge, but it is also an honesty that is vulnerable and not defensive. (Honesty can be a defence when it is one person telling another the difficulty they have with the other or what is wrong with the other, whilst not being able to acknowledge as openly that which they appreciate, value and respect of the other.) The honesty of intimacy is a sharing of oneself, one's opinions and feelings in a way that is welcoming to the other while staying open and available to listen fully and attend to the other's truth as well as one's own.

These meditative moments, when the world stands still, are perhaps more likely to occur in the quiet of the mountains or at loving points of human contact but they can also occur in the midst of bustle and turmoil. A revelatory moment in the middle of a blazing row or a shaft of light in a busy street may also bring us a moment of contemplative awareness which halts our rush for a moment in time and holds us transfixed with a sense of mystery and of something that is much greater hidden behind the surface of things.

Nourishing our souls is important if we are to be able to open our hearts to others – both to give and to receive love. Sometimes it is assumed that such nourishment automatically takes place in religious rituals and services. It is just as likely to take place elsewhere and rituals can become dry and empty unless they are imbued with meaning and a sense of the sacred.

For many, relaxation and guided visualisations may be their initiation to meditation. This may be done in meditation groups or even by listening to appropriate tapes. During a guided relaxation exercise, images are suggested for meditation. Such images include visiting a peaceful place, going through the scenes of a parable or a story of healing from the Bible, the images of water, such as a crystal clear stream washing over one with the suggestion that it is taking away all that needs to be discarded and renewing and replenishing us with its life and vitality. A different form of introduction might include material for reflection and then a time of quietness.

Following the stream of consciousness that flows through us can also provide an introductory encounter. For this, you begin to name silently or out loud whatever you are aware of. In this way you begin to track your attention. This can be practised alone or with another, if you can trust them and yourself with whatever comes to mind.

Just say out loud 'Now I am aware . . .' For example, 'Now I am aware. . . of the wind rustling, of the dog moving, of a tightness in my neck, of taking a deep breath, of wondering what time it is, of my foot, of feeling a bit shaky, of a tightness in my belly, of wondering about my child, of . . . blank, of having let my thoughts drift, of returning to the exercise, of wondering how long I can continue, of . . . a deep breath, of . . . '

Having practised out loud a bit one can then more easily perhaps do it silently. This is also an exercise which comes from Gestalt therapy and is described by John O. Stevens in his book, *Awareness*. This awareness exercise can be an introduction to meditation because many meditative practices suggest just following the stream of one's thoughts. Whatever we choose to focus our attention upon: breath, our flow of consciousness, a candle flame or another object – our thoughts will wander. This is part of the process and when we realise this has happened it is appropriate simply to return our attention to that which we are choosing to focus upon.

The central process in meditation practice is to focus attention so we can focus on the rise and fall of our breath, on an external object, or on a mantra or on a physical movement, as in Tai C'hi. Specific exercises are suggested by different schools, such as different breathing practices or mantras which may be appropriate to one's own beliefs.

A mantra may be a particular word or sound or it may be a phrase. This word, or phrase, is continually repeated. Such a mantra may also be used like a chant; many chants are used for contemplative prayer or for meditation. If you are inclined to have difficulty in disengaging your thoughts, a reflective style of mantra – which would be a meaningful sentence – may be more distracting than contemplative. This is because you may be drawn to reflect on all the different aspects and directions the sentence will take rather than deepen your consciousness. Ultimately such reflections may bring you to a deeper consciousness but initially they may serve to hold your attention at an intellectual level – a level which you need to move beyond.

Often, consciously or subconsciously, we fear to enter the stillness. Uncomfortable feelings may emerge, often simply because they are unfamiliar. Just allow the discomfort and allow yourself to be present to whatever feelings, images or thoughts emerge, then let them go and return your attention to the focus point or mantra and this will enable you to continue.

People sometimes express the fear that evil, or the devil, will be let in if you allow the space. The implication is that if we don't keep tight control of our minds at all times, the devil will overpower us. Paradoxically, the more we exercise such control, the more the so-called negative aspects of our personalities have to be suppressed. Such suppression means that, given space, things we don't want to know about ourselves may well surface. These things are not evil but we may judge them so. Such shadow aspects of ourselves are better shown the light of day. It takes the intensity out of them and prevents us from pro-jecting all our 'bad' feelings on to others and pretending to ourselves that we are purer than driven snow. We are humans and these hidden aspects of ourselves are often the grit that is transformed through human encounter and the alchemical process of love.

We can get stuck in meditation. At such times, for example, we may feel unable to meditate without knowing the reason, and the experience of meditation may have changed from what is familiar. This is when a good teacher may be called for, or therapy may be appropriate. Our human history deeply affects our relationship with others and the way we approach the divine. Sometimes it is only by working through our human distress that we can continue on our spiritual journey. Of course these two cannot in fact be separated – that is the nature of humanity. Sometimes it is appropriate to journey in ways more obviously spiritual and at other times we are called on to acknowledge and deal with the difficulties within us that alienate us from our capacity for love.

Prayer is the way we communicate with God. Much of

the prayer we were taught in western cultures concentrated on the way we talk to God and did not emphasise the ways we could open ourselves to hear the voice of God. This book, in essence, has been about accessing the divine connection – the connection to love. We do this by presenting ourselves to God, by telling our story, by sharing our fears, by asking for guidance, by expressing our gratitude and celebrating the wonder of love. We also do it by learning to open our eyes and ears to divine presence. This may be through prayer and meditation, through nature, through relationships or through paying attention to synchronistic connections that seem to regularly occur when we are on our path.

The religious paths of the wisdom religions have always been deeply embedded in nature. Wisdom religions are the religions of native peoples whose ways were so often misunderstood by the Christian missionaries who travelled far and wide to convert people to Christianity. Sadly, working out of the theology of the time, these missionaries often tried to convert native people to the western social ideals that seemed to them to be the expression of Christianity rather than to the core of Christianity. In this way, they actually drew them away from the deeply connected spiritual paths they were following from which we in the west have so much to learn. Different religions shed different light on aspects of divine love and Christians did have something to offer but also much to learn which could have enhanced our own Christian understanding. There is always something to be learned from other people's religion.

Now, when an individualistic and paternalistic culture

has taken us to dangerous extremes, we are suddenly realising the importance of spiritual paths embedded in nature. Westerners, who often have great difficulty in relating to the Christianity of their own culture, are returning to the leaders of native wisdom in desperation to learn how to live in 'right relation' with the earth and all her inhabitants, including humans. Native leaders have despaired at our rape of the earth and our disrespect for her bounty, have seen us destroying not only their world (most of which is already destroyed) but the whole world. To people whose culture and religion require that they 'walk their talk', Christian behaviour does not seem consistent with talk of a God of love. Our relationship to the natural world of which we are part portrays only too clearly our alienation from God and, in particular, from the feminine aspect of God which calls us to remember earth as mother.

Deep ecology is the phrase being used to describe the spiritual right relationship we need so desperately to recover with the earth and other inhabitants who share life with us. We have to learn to see ourselves as part of the living planet rather than people who constantly try to control and pillage nature. In alienating ourselves from our bodies, from feelings and from all that is and was we have also alienated ourselves from nature. The natural world in particular often awakens our sense of mystery and awe. Many people describe experiences in nature if they are asked about religious experiences but such experiences have often been undermined rather than valued by our western religions.

If we are to return to love, if we are to nourish

ourselves sufficiently to be able to love others, we have to return to our awareness of the sacredness of nature and everyday life. When we take from the earth it must always be in the context of giving something back. We have to learn, from indigenous people, to think of the generations ahead and to prepare for them whenever we take for ourselves.

In addition, we need to learn to pay attention to nature and to what it has to teach us. We need to learn to listen intuitively to her voice – the rustle of the leaves, the patter of the rain, the flow of rivers, to know when she is crying out for attention and to give it. If we were able to live truly in an aware relationship with the rest of nature around us we would be naturally more open, more meditative, more connected and more aware of belonging. With this would come the sense of the love that mother earth nurtures us with every day and also, of course, the love within us that springs from the source just as the source of a well is fed from the depths below.

In *Listening to Nature*, Joseph Cornell quotes Tanaka Shozo as saying 'The care of rivers is not a question of rivers, but of the human heart'. In the same book, Cornell reminds us 'With love comes understanding and the motivation for right action.' When we return to the source of life and rest in love, we know that right action is the only way we can live and remain true to our deepest selves. Such action requires us to act justly and requires us to nurture the planet which gives us life.

11

THE WAY OF LOVE

The Tao that can be told is not the etermal Tao.

These are the translated words of Lao Tsu in the *Tao Te Ching* Book of Wisdom written many hundreds of years before Christ. (Translation by Gia-Fu Feng and Jane English.) Similarly, the love that can be written about is not love. A picture described is not the picture. Beauty written about is not beauty itself.

To write about love immediately limits the very thing one is writing about. However, we talk about it, describe it, talk its language, imagine it, the love we are talking about is not love itself. Love itself is always greater and always richer than that which can be expressed.

Lao Tsu wrote about the Tao – which can be roughly translated as 'The Way' – as the living energy of the universe. We are in tune with that energy – on The Way – or else off course. When we are in tune, then doing is not doing, making happen is in the way of allowing. In other words, when we are living in harmony with the essence of the universe, with our own essence, then we no longer need to strive, push or act out of will alone, because just as the rain falls and the sun shines, then things happen apparently of their own accord in the appropriate way and each piece falls naturally into place in the moving jigsaw of life.

Taoism does not have a dualistic view of the universe. Hence the sign known as the sign of peace in the west: the circle is divided into black and white halves with a circle of white in the black half and a circle of black in the white half, signifying that there is always black in the white and white in the black and that every polarity has its opposite polarity expressed in it.

In other words, the way of love is not always sweetness and light. Ultimately it is a way that is beyond our full comprehension. It includes our struggle and darkness as well as moments of illumination and joy. To be on The Way is to be in touch with as much of ourselves as possible and to open ourselves to the full experience of life. Such an encounter engages the grit of life. It does not shy away from darkness but brings it into light, engaging it in the alchemical process that can transform. It engages us in the alchemical process of living and love in a way that can transform us.

This is an ongoing process. The process is all there is. In our lifetime we can grieve our alienation and in the process more closely identify with our core of love but we do not journey to arrive at perfection.

This is because we will never attain perfect love – at least not on this earth – because, paradoxically, we are perfect already. Perfectly imperfect – part of the alchemical process, beings in the process of becoming, these are the descriptions most applicable to our situation.

These things are difficult to hear if we are intent on learning to be 'good' so as to reap divine commendation.

The challenge is to accept the message that is already there – we are loved by God as we are. Our limited experiences of love, which have nearly always been conditional, make this difficult to take in. The more we can accept the complexity of ourselves and the ambiguities of our situation, the more we seem to grow in love. Having compassion for ourselves we need to accept ourselves as perfectly imperfect. Having such compassion, we can expect no more of anyone else. Hence we move toward accepting others with fewer conditions, with more love.

As we align ourselves more with the path, the struggle diminishes and surrender becomes easier. We surrender to what we are and return more to the centre of ourselves and to a more contented way of being.

When we can live in a centred way – at least some of the time – and listen to ourselves and the things around us, we often become aware of the way things can connect up 'coincidentally'. Synchronicity is the term used by Jung to describe the amazing coincidences that can occur in the objective world when events coincide, or connect, with that which is happening in our own psyche.

Simple things may occur, like someone telephoning you out of the blue about something that is preoccupying your attention. When we begin to attend intuitively to the world around us, such coincidences can become part of the normality of everyday life.

Writing this book involved several such experiences, including being asked to write it in the first place. Some related to oracles. In recent years many books have been published which could be broadly defined as oracular. Some, such as the *I Ching*, are ancient books of wisdom which were consulted in particular ways for guidance. In the past these oracles were consulted with reverence and serious attention was paid to the readings received. This is strange for those of us brought up in current orthodox religious ways. Nowadays, new forms of oracle are being written and published.

When we suspend judgement and allow ourselves to be open in a meditative way to guidance from wherever it comes, the possibilities may surprise us. We need to 'listen' intuitively to such forms of guidance, recognising that our own level of self-knowledge and awareness of the issues influences our ability to interpret what arises. The following is a description of this process by the author in diary form, written about half-way through the process of completing this book.

Yesterday I was looking at the Animal Medicine cards, (Sams and Carson, 1988) setting them out so that my husband could take one. After we had looked at his card and read what the notes said about it, I discovered a card on the floor. In tune with the spirit of the thing, I decided that this card might have a message for me and that I would look in the book accompanying the cards. The card was a snake, subtitled 'transmutation'. A lot of its message is about shedding its skin and the need for surrendering things of the past. The power of snake medicine is the power of creation, for it embodies sexuality, psychic energy, alchemy, reproduction and ascension (or immortality).

The transmutation of the life-death-rebirth cycle

is exemplified by the shedding of Snake's skin.

'If you have chosen this symbol, there is a need within you to transmute some thought, action or desire, so that wholeness can be achieved.'

I see this card while I am at a low ebb, wondering about writing a book – whether I really have anything to say, whether I can do it, whether it would be damaging to me to put it out, whether it is just repetitive nonsense.

Another thing is preoccupying me on this day. Six days ago I scalded my hand and all week I have been watching the skin peel without thinking about it as skin peeling. On the morning I received the card, I was wondering whether I ought to go to the doctor, because it seemed that every time the new skin grew, it peeled away again and I have a messy looking patch of layers of skin peeling and a redness and it looked rather dried-up. So on this day I was massaging in cream, trying to keep it supple so that the skin would last, something I have been doing for a few days without obvious success.

Some hours after receiving the card, I suddenly saw my burn in a new way. I looked at the skin peeling and I wondered if it had anything to teach me.

I was feeling particularly low that evening when a friend arrived unexpectedly, to my great relief and delight. Once again, I was feeling low about the book and seriously questioning whether I should be doing it at all. I enjoyed her visit and went to bed late. Still preoccupied with the book, I sought some comfort for myself. I drew a Rune stone. These are stones that were used as an oracle by the Vikings. In the preface to *The Book of Runes,* Martin Raynor says: 'Oracles do not absolve you from responsibility for selecting your future, but rather direct your attention towards those inner choices that may be the most important element in determining that future.'

I had drawn Rune Number 4 – to do with separation, retreat, inheritance. 'Now is a time of separating paths. Old skin must be shed, outmoded relationships discarded. When this Rune appears in a spread, a peeling away is called for.' And further on: 'whether it is your attachment to your position in society, to the work you do, or even to your beliefs about your own nature, the separation called for now will free you to become more truly who you are.'

I went to sleep feeling assured that somehow I was going to learn something. The next morning I woke early and I was reflecting on the shedding of skin and the messages of the previous day. I wondered if it was to tell me to retreat from the book. Then I realised that the process of writing this book has real energy and life in it. We shed dead skin, not the skin that is forming.

Following my apparently idle reflections, as one often does lying in bed in the morning, I reflected on the way I consult the oracles of *The Book of Runes* and the Medicine cards. I thought about how some people see such actions as unChristian. I thought about how such consultations can help one to reflect upon something, discovering important aspects of what is happening in one's life and of how much they have encouraged me at times. I thought of how great it is that God speaks to us in these ways and how compatible with Christianity this process is. Following this line of thought, I decided to consult the Bible and so I allowed it fall open and with my eyes closed, I selected a page and took my time, to feel my way to what seemed the right place.

It was open at St John's Gospel and talked of how many of the disciples peeled away when Christ talked to them about his body as the bread of life.

Unless you eat my flesh and drink my blood . . .
Unless you partake of the life I offer . . .

John 6:54

Following these reflections, I began to think about Thomas Moore's phrase that is the epigraph to this book: 'Love is an alchemical process in which we are the material to be transmuted'. I started to repeat the phrase like a mantra, giving emphasis to the different words and different intonations to the sentence. It struck me that this phrase also expresses the whole Christian message: Christ's death on the cross and his Resurrection, the Eucharist, all teaching the transmuting power of love and much more besides.

My mini-thesaurus didn't have the word transmute, but it did have the words 'transformation' or 'transform' and both of them gave transmute or transmutation as an alternative. The antonym of transformation turned out to be preservation and the antonym of transform 'preserve'. So much of the time we try to preserve religious teachings, preserve the status quo, preserve ourselves. Life cannot be preserved, it can only be lived. That which is preserved will die unless there is life in it.

'Love is an alchemical process in which we are the material to be transmuted'. Life is an alchemical process in which we are the material to be transmuted. Maybe indeed life is. I think however, that life has this potential whereas love *is* indeed an alchemical process in which we are the material to be transmuted. Love is the alchemical process with which we must connect.

That morning the scar from my scald was healing nicely. There was nice new pink skin around the edges of the wound and although the centre was still red, it had a healthy glow. It was after this experience that the core theme of the book became more focused and the title emerged.

It is not only through intuitively paying attention to the wisdom that oracles or our health may offer that we can learn to listen to the inner counsellor. Many apparent coincidences have been described that link natural occurrences with internal processes, such as a bird or a butterfly appearing at incredibly significant moments and then repeating the coincidence by appearing again when the event is recalled. Sometimes a much deeper significance is discovered when time elapses and further reflection on the events can take place. Why this happens is not important here. It is simply valuable to record that such occurrences take place and may be much more commonplace than is assumed.

When we pay attention, when we allow ourselves to be present, not only with our thinking but also with all of our senses and feelings, we learn there are many significant ways of learning about the world. Opening ourselves to coincidences and paying attention to them and to directions they may suggest is another way of finding the way on our path.

Our capacity for conscious thought and intelligence is critical and must not be rejected. But our capacity for intuitive knowing, for feeling and for sensing has been neglected and needs to be recovered, both to balance rational intelligence and because this kind of knowing adds a huge dimension to our capacity for understanding the world in which we live. Ignoring these aspects of ourselves means blinkering our potential vision and limiting our perceptions.

Such capacities are critical for art but also for the vision which often inspires scientists to undertake the necessary empirical research to validate their knowledge. Our ability to be present, in every way, is critical to our ability to find and follow our way. It is through such avenues that we come to a deeper sense of knowing, so that we no longer question the existence of God or the Goddess or Love or Spirit, but come to wonder instead how on earth we manage consistently to alienate ourselves so completely from the source of our being, from our ground, from divine goodness – from love and from life itself.

SELECTED BIBLIOGRAPHY

BOOKS

Abrams, Jeremiah. *Reclaiming the Inner Child*. Mandala, 1991.

Blum, Ralph. *The Book of Runes* (accompanied by Rune Stones). New York: Oracle Books, St Martin's Press, 1932; revised 1982.

Bradshaw, John. *Homecoming*. London: Piatkus, 1985.

Broadella, David. *Wilhelm Reich: The Evolution of his Work*. London, Boston and Henley: Arkana, 1985.

Capra, Fritjof and David Steindl-Rast with Thomas Matus. *Belonging to the Universe: Explorations on the Frontiers of Science and Spirituality*. San Francisco: Harper, 1991.

————————. *The Turning Point: Science, Society and the Rising Culture*. London: Wildwood House, 1982.

————————. *The Tao of Physics*. London: Flamingo, 1976

————————. *Uncommon Wisdom: Conversations with Remarkable People*. London: Flamingo, 1989.

Cornell, Joseph. *Listening to Nature*. USA: Dawn Publications, 1994.

Cox, Harvey. *Many Mansions: a Christian's Encounter with Other Faiths*. London: Collins, 1988.

Feng, Gia-Fu and Jane English. *Lao-tzu*. London: Wildwood House, 1973.

Gallegos, E. S. *The Personal Totem Pole: Animal Imagery, the Chakras, and Psychotherapy*. Santa Fe: Moon Bear Press, 1987, 2nd edition 1990.

————————. *Animals of the Four Windows*. Santa Fe:

Moon Bear Press, 1992.

Goldber Lerner, Harriet. *The Dance of Deception: Pretending and Truth-telling in Women's Lives.* New York: Harper Collins, 1993.

Griffiths, Fr Bede. The New C*reation in Christ – Meditation and Community.* London: Darton Longman and Todd, 1992.

Grof, Stanislav. *Ancient Wisdom and Modern Science.* New York: State University of New York Press, 1984.

————————. Beyond the *Brain.* New York: State University of New York Press, 1985.

————————. Realms of *the Human Unconscious.* London: Souvenir Press, 1979.

Jeffares, Susan. *Dare to Connect.* London: Piatkus, 1992.

Jung, C. G.. *Jung on Alchemy.* London: Routledge, 1995.

————————. *Synchronicity.* London: Ark Paperbacks, 1985.

Keleman, Stanley. *The Human Ground: Sexuality, Self and Society.* Berkeley, California: Center Press, 1975.

Lowen, Alexander MD. *Bioenergetics: The Revolutionary Therapy that Uses the Language of the Body to Heal the Problems of the Mind.* Harmondsworth: Penguin, 1975.

Moore, Thomas. *Soul Mates.* Shaftesbury, Dorset: Element Books, 1994.

Reich, Wilhelm. *The Function of the Orgasm.* New York: Pocket Books, 1973.

Rowan, John. *The Reality Game.* London: Routledge, Keegan and Paul, 1983.

————————. *The Transpersonal:* Psychotherapy and *Counselling.* London and New York: Routledge, 1993.

Sams, Jamie and David Carson. *Medicine Cards.* Santa Fe: Bear and Co, 1988.

Satir, Virginia. *Peoplemaking.* USA: Souvenir Press, 1972.

Simonton, C., M. Simonton and J. Creighton. *Getting Well Again.* New York: Bantam Books, 1978.

Smith, Cyprian OSB. *The Way of Paradox.* London: Longman and Todd, 1987.

Stevens, John O. *Awareness.* Utah: Real People Press, 1971.

Tatlebaum, Judy. *The Courage to Grieve.* London: Cedar, 1980.

Watts, Alan (with the collaboration of Al Chung-Liang Huang). *Tao: The Watercourse Way.* Harmondsworth: Penguin, 1975.

Welwood, John (ed). *Awakening the Heart: East/West Approaches to Psychotherapy and the Healing Relationship.* Boulder: Shambala, 1983.

————————. *Journey of the Heart.* London: Mandala, 1990.

Whitfield, Charles. *Healing the Child Within.* Florida: Health Communications, 1989.

Wilber, Ken. *Grace and Grit: Spirtuality and Healing in the Life of Treya Killam Wilber.* Boston: Shambala, 1989; Dublin: Gill and Macmillan, 1994.

————————. *The Atman Project.* USA: Quest, Wheaton, 1980.

————————. *The Spectrum of Consciousness.* USA: The Theosophical Publishing House, 1977.

OTHER MATERIAL

Rogers, Carl. 'Personally Speaking'. Dublin: RTE, 1985. A television interview with John Masterson.

Whyte, David. 'Close to Home, Ecological Imagination'. Lecture delivered at Thirteenth Conference of the International Transpersonal Association, Killarney, Ireland, May 1994.